STOP ANXIETY NOW

90-Second Tools to Smash Panic, Rewire Your Brain & Own Every Day

by

Dr. Ava Kingsley, PsyD

**Copyright 2025 Dr. Ava Kingsley, PsyD.
All rights reserved.**

No part of this book may be reproduced in any form or by any electronic or mechanical means including information storage and retrieval systems, without permission in writing from the author. The only exception is by a reviewer, who may quote short excerpts in a review.

Although the author and publisher have made every effort to ensure that the information in this book was correct at press time, the author and publisher do not assume and hereby disclaim any liability to any party for any loss, damage, or disruption caused by errors or omissions, whether such errors or omissions result from negligence, accident, or any other cause.

This publication is designed to provide accurate and authoritative information with regard to the subject matter covered. It is sold with the understanding that the publisher is not engaged in rendering professional services. If legal advice or other expert assistance is required, the services of a competent professional should be sought.

The fact that an organization or website is referred to in this work as a citation and/or a potential source of further information does not mean that the author or the publisher endorses the information the organization or website may provide or recommendations it may make.

Please remember that Internet websites listed in this work may have changed or disappeared between when this work was written and when it is read.

Stop Anxiety Now: 90-Second Tools to Smash Panic, Rewire Your Brain & Own Every Day

Table of Contents

INTRODUCTION _____ 7

CHAPTER 1 _____ 13
Understanding Anxiety Quickly and Clearly

    Anxiety 101: What's Really Going On in Your Brain

    The Panic Loop: How Fear Hijacks Your System

    The 90-Second Window: Science Behind the Method

    Why You Don't Need to "Fix" Yourself to Feel Better

CHAPTER 2 _____ 35
The 90-Second Tools for Instant Relief

    Tool 1: Grounding in the Moment (The 5-4-3-2-1 Reset)

    Tool 2: Tactical Breathing (Calm in 60 Seconds)

    Tool 3: Instant Reframe (Shift the Thought Spiral)

    Tool 4: Tense and Release (Body-Based Relief)

    Tool 5: The Cold Reset (Activate Your Vagus Nerve)

    Tool 6: "What If" to "What Is" (Stop Future Tripping)

    Tool 7: The 90-Second Journal (Track and Train Your Brain)

    Tool 8: Micro-Movement for Maximum Calm

    Tool 9: The 1-Minute Mindset Reset

    Tool 10: Emergency Exit Plan (For High-Intensity Moments)

CHAPTER 3 _____ **89**
Rewiring the Brain for Long-Term Change
    The Brain Is a Pattern Machine: How to Rewire It
    Neuroplasticity in Action: Small Shifts, Big Wins
    Build a Daily 5-Minute Practice That Actually Sticks
    Sleep, Food, and Screens: Hidden Anxiety Triggers
    How to Talk to Anxiety Instead of Fighting It

CHAPTER 4 _____ **115**
Owning Every Day with Confidence
    Morning Routines for an Anxiety-Proof Day
    Handling Social Anxiety in Real Time
    Anxiety at Work: Tools for Focus and Confidence
    When You're Not Feeling Strong—Use the "Borrowed Strength" Hack
    Living Bigger Than Anxiety: Redefining "Brave"

You're Not Broken—You're Building Something Stronger

Introduction

Anxiety has a way of sneaking into your life when you least expect it. It often arrives without warning, hijacking your thoughts and filling your body with tension. For many who battle anxiety or panic attacks, it can feel like an endless cycle of fear, overwhelm, and frustration. You might find yourself searching for solutions that work—methods that provide quick relief and tools you can use anytime, anywhere. This book aims to be exactly that kind of resource: a practical, science-backed guide to managing anxiety on your own terms.

Rather than diving into long-term therapy or complicated treatments that require a lot of time or money, **Conquer Anxiety Now** focuses on fast-acting techniques you can use in those critical moments when anxiety tries to take over. These aren't just random tips; every tool in this book is rooted in neuroscience and psychology, designed to interrupt the panic cycle within 90 seconds. Yes, you read that right—90 seconds. That window is where change happens, where you can reclaim control, even in the middle of a panic attack or a flood of anxious thoughts.

Living with anxiety can make simple daily tasks suddenly feel overwhelming. You're not alone if you've felt exhausted from trying to "just calm down" or frustrated because traditional advice seemed out of reach or ineffective. Anxiety isn't about a lack of willpower or strength; it's about how your brain and body react to stress and perceived threats. That's why this book won't ask you to "fix" yourself in some broad, vague sense. Instead, it offers clear, actionable strategies to help rewire your brain's response patterns and build your resilience one step at a time.

In the pages ahead, you'll discover how anxiety works beneath the surface—without getting lost in confusing jargon. But the main focus will always be on what YOU can do, fast and effectively. Whether it's a sudden wave of panic while sitting in a meeting or simmering anxiety that just won't quit before bedtime, these tools give you the ability to break free and find calm.

What sets this approach apart is its simplicity and accessibility. There's no need for special equipment, lengthy meditation retreats, or expensive therapy sessions. You can practice most of these techniques right where you are—at home, at work, or even on the go. This means you can start using the tools immediately, without delay.

As we move through this book, keep in mind that managing anxiety isn't about being perfect or erasing all nervous feelings. Anxiety will always be a part of life for many people. Instead, it's about learning to step out of its shadow and live more fully despite it. This mindset shift—from feeling controlled by anxiety to owning your response to it—is central to lasting change.

Understanding that change is possible is the first step toward freedom. Many who struggle with anxiety have tried countless "quick fixes" that don't last or leave them feeling worse. The methods in this book cut through that noise. They're built on research and real-world experience, offering a clear path from panic to peace without overwhelming you with too much information at once.

At the core of this book is compassion—for yourself and your journey. Anxiety isn't a personal failure or something you simply "should" overcome with effort alone. It's a natural response that your brain is wired for, sometimes turned up too high. By learning to work with your brain's natural patterns instead of against them, you'll develop tools that actually fit your life, your schedule, and your needs.

Each chapter builds on the last, but the focus here in the Introduction is setting the stage. This is where you get grounded in the concept that faster relief is possible, and it doesn't have to be complicated. It's also about mindset: seeing anxiety not as an enemy but as a signal from your brain that something needs your attention. Approaching it with curiosity rather than judgment opens the door to real progress.

By the end of this book, you'll have a toolbox full of immediate strategies plus longer-term practices to rewire your brain for calm and confidence. You'll understand the science behind why these techniques work and how to apply them most effectively in your daily life. More importantly, you'll reclaim a sense of control over your anxiety rather than feeling like it controls you.

This introduction is an invitation to begin that journey—one short step at a time. You deserve to experience life with less fear and more freedom. It's not about eliminating every anxious thought but about learning how to manage them so they don't run the show. The tools ahead are designed to give you that power, fast.

Whether you're new to anxiety management or have tried other methods before, this book offers a fresh approach grounded in the latest research and practical wisdom. You don't have to wait for the anxiety to subside on its own or hope that time will "fix" things. With a little practice, you can break the panic cycle quickly and build a foundation for lasting change.

Remember, this isn't a journey you have to take alone or feel helpless in. The methods here are based on human brain science—meaning your brain itself can change, adapt, and grow calmer with the right guidance. It's empowering to know that even when anxiety feels overwhelming, you have tools within reach to calm your body, steer your thoughts, and steady your emotions.

Let this book be the first step in taking back your peace of mind. Anxiety may be part of your experience, but it doesn't have to define your life. With the right strategies, you can smash panic, rewire your brain, and own every day on your own terms.

Chapter 1
UNDERSTANDING ANXIETY QUICKLY AND CLEARLY

Anxiety often hits like a sudden storm, and understanding what's really happening inside your brain can be a game changer to managing it effectively; it's not just feeling nervous or stressed but a complex survival mechanism that sometimes goes into overdrive, hijacking your body's natural responses and trapping you in a feedback loop of fear that feels impossible to escape; the good news is, this reaction doesn't mean you're broken or weak—it's simply how your brain is wired to protect you, even if it feels overwhelming, and recognizing this opens the door to using quick, science-backed methods that interrupt this cycle and help you regain control within seconds, setting the stage for lasting relief and resilience.

DR. AVA KINGSLEY, PSYD

ANXIETY 101: WHAT'S REALLY GOING ON IN YOUR BRAIN

Anxiety can feel like an out-of-control storm brewing inside your head, but understanding what's happening in your brain can help you take back the reins. When you're anxious, your body isn't just reacting randomly—it's actually engaging a very old, automatic survival system wired deeply into your nervous system. This system is designed to protect you from harm, but sometimes, it gets tricked into sounding the alarm even when there's no real threat. That's where anxiety begins.

At the root of anxiety is a part of your brain called the amygdala. Think of the amygdala as the brain's alarm center. It constantly scans your environment for danger—even if it's just a subtle hint rather than a clear threat. Once it detects something it interprets as dangerous, it sends an urgent signal that activates your body's fight, flight, or freeze response. Your heart races, muscles tense up, and your breathing speeds up in preparation to face or flee the perceived danger. This response evolved to keep you alive in life-threatening situations, but nowadays it often kicks in unnecessarily.

Next, the hippocampus comes into play. This part of the brain helps you store memories, especially those tied to emotions. It helps your brain remember situations similar to the current one and judge whether they were safe or dangerous. When the hippocampus associates past experiences with fear, it can amplify your anxiety by making current events feel more threatening than they really are. That's why sometimes you might feel anxious in situations that shouldn't be frightening but remind you subconsciously of something stressful from your past.

Meanwhile, the prefrontal cortex—the brain's decision-maker and logical thinker—tries to calm things down. It steps in to assess the situation, weigh the real risk, and plan your next move. But here's the catch: during moments of acute anxiety, the prefrontal cortex often gets overwhelmed by the amygdala's rush of alert signals. This means your ability to reason clearly sometimes takes a backseat, leaving your instinctual fear response in control. You might find yourself trapped in a loop where anxious thoughts keep escalating, even if you logically know there's no immediate danger.

This tug of war between the amygdala and prefrontal cortex is why anxiety can feel so confusing. Your body is preparing to escape a threat your mind can't quite pinpoint or even recognize as real. It's a survival response gone haywire, putting your brain and body on high alert when you really just need to relax.

Often, the anxious brain gets stuck in hypervigilance, meaning it's constantly on the lookout for threats, no matter how minor. That's why everyday scenarios—like crowded rooms, work deadlines, or even sitting quietly—can seem overwhelming and hazardous. Your brain can't easily differentiate between real dangers and stressors your mind has blown out of proportion. This results in persistent worry and physical symptoms like a pounding heart, nausea, or dizziness.

It's important to realize that anxiety isn't a personal failing or a character flaw. It's your brain working overtime to keep you safe, but it's using outdated strategies that don't fit well with modern life. The more you fight or resist anxiety, the more power you give it, because it thrives on avoidance and fear. The key is learning how to shift the brain's response, so you can quiet the alarm and regain control.

Neurotransmitters, the brain's chemical messengers, also play a big role here. Chemicals like serotonin, gamma-aminobutyric acid (GABA), and dopamine help regulate mood, calm the nervous system, and balance anxiety levels. When these neurotransmitters are out of balance—due to stress, genetics, lifestyle, or chemical imbalances—the brain struggles to maintain emotional equilibrium. Understanding this helps demystify why anxiety can be particularly intense at times and why treatments that support chemical balance can make such a difference.

One of the fascinating things about your brain is its plasticity—its ability to change and adapt throughout life. The anxious brain isn't fixed. With consistent practice and the right tools, you can rewire these automatic anxiety patterns and create new neural pathways that promote calm and resilience. You don't have to be stuck with that constant alarm ringing inside your head.

STOP ANXIETY NOW

To sum it up, anxiety arises when your brain's primitive threat-detection system activates unnecessarily. The amygdala lights up like an alarm bell, your hippocampus stacks past worries into the mix, and your prefrontal cortex struggles to regain control. This leads to the intense physical and emotional sensations that define anxiety. Knowing what's going on behind the scenes is the first powerful step toward breaking free.

When you begin to understand anxiety at a brain level, you stop blaming yourself and start embracing strategies designed to calm those overactive alarm signals. Think of it as learning the language of your brain, then using that knowledge to press "reset" in moments of panic or worry. Instead of feeling like a prisoner to anxiety, you start reclaiming your power over it.

This is where rapid interventions and practical tools come in. They don't just distract you; they actively engage your brain's regulatory systems to interrupt the cycle of anxiety before it spirals out of control. The next chapters will dive into these science-backed techniques that work with your brain, rather than against it, to help you feel grounded fast.

Remember, your brain's anxiety response was meant to keep you safe. Now, you'll learn how to tell your brain, "Thanks for the heads-up, but I've got this." Because once you truly understand what's going on inside your brain, you

DR. AVA KINGSLEY, PSYD

gain the clarity and motivation to change your relationship with anxiety—and, ultimately, change your life.

THE PANIC LOOP: HOW FEAR HIJACKS YOUR SYSTEM

When anxiety strikes, it often feels like your body and mind have teamed up against you. This isn't just in your head—there's a real, biological process driving these sensations. What you're experiencing is what we call the panic loop, a cycle where fear takes control and hijacks your entire system. Once caught in this loop, calming down can seem impossible. Understanding how this loop works helps you break free faster and regain control almost immediately.

Think of the panic loop as a feedback system gone haywire. Your brain constantly scans the environment, looking for danger. When it detects a threat—real or perceived—it triggers a fear response to get you ready to act. This response is meant to protect you, activating your fight, flight, or freeze instincts. Those rapid heartbeats, sweating, shallow breathing, and racing thoughts? They're your body's way of preparing for an emergency. But with anxiety, this system misfires, trapping you in a loop where fear feeds on itself.

The moment your brain detects danger, it sends signals to your body through the nervous system. Your adrenaline spikes, your muscles tense, and your breathing quickens. Even if there's no real threat around, your body reacts as if there's imminent danger. This heightened physical state intensifies your perception of fear, which then loops back to your brain, amplifying the original anxiety signals. The result? A spiraling interaction between mind and body that keeps your panic going without letting up.

What's tricky about the panic loop is that it's automatic and fast. You don't consciously choose to feel anxious; your brain's fear system kicks in on its own. It operates below the level of conscious thought, so telling yourself to "just calm down" often doesn't work. Instead, the more you fight the fear with resistance or worry, the stronger the panic loop becomes. It's like trying to stop a spinning top by grabbing its outer edge—pulling harder only makes it spin faster.

At the heart of this cycle is the amygdala, a small almond-shaped part of your brain that processes emotions and survival instincts. When the amygdala senses a threat, it triggers the release of stress hormones like adrenaline and cortisol. This emotional alarm system prioritizes immediate survival over rational thinking, pushing your body into a hyper-alert state. This response is great if you're escaping a real predator, but it's exhausting and unnecessary when the fear is based only on your thoughts or misinterpretations.

The panic loop also hijacks your prefrontal cortex, the brain region responsible for reasoning and decision-making. Under stress, the amygdala essentially takes the wheel, limiting your ability to think clearly or rationally. This explains why, in a panic attack, it's difficult to challenge fearful thoughts or focus on calming strategies. Your rational mind is temporarily overpowered by the primal fear circuits, making the experience feel overwhelming and uncontrollable.

Physically, the panic loop causes a cascade of symptoms that reinforce the feeling of danger. For example, rapid breathing can lead to lightheadedness or tingling sensations, which your brain interprets as more evidence that something is wrong. This fuels more fear, sending you deeper into the cycle. Your heart pounding or chest tightness feels alarming, prompting more panic. It's a vicious circle where physical sensations and emotional reactions feed off each other, escalating quickly if left unchecked.

Understanding that this loop is a biological process—not a sign of personal weakness—can be incredibly freeing. When you realize that your brain and body are reacting the way they were designed to, it's easier to stop blaming yourself. Anxiety isn't about "losing control"; it's about your survival system running in overdrive without a real threat. Once you shift this perspective, you create space to work with your body and brain instead of against them.

Breaking the panic loop requires interrupting the cycle at any point—calming the body, shifting attention, or changing the meaning of your thoughts. Because the loop is so fast, these interruptions need to happen quickly, often within seconds. The good news? You're already equipped with tools to do just that, and many of these tools work by leveraging your body's natural processes to downshift the fear response.

DR. AVA KINGSLEY, PSYD

One of the key points to remember is that the panic loop is not permanent. It's temporary and will subside if you don't fuel it with more fear or resistance. Although it may feel like panic could last forever, the system resets once your brain senses safety. Your goal becomes to help your brain recognize safety again, shutting down the emergency signals so you can return to a calm, balanced state.

It's important to recognize that fear, at its core, is trying to keep you alive. It doesn't care that it's making life hard. The panic loop exists because your brain sees any change or uncertainty as a potential threat, even when that's not true. Learning how to spot this trick gives you power over the cycle. When you catch yourself spiraling, you can remind your nervous system that you're safe right now.

Because the panic loop affects the nervous system first, strategies that calm your body often work best to shut it down early. Slowing your breathing or focusing on physical sensations helps break the feedback loop between body and mind. This kind of grounding technique interrupts the system, signaling to your brain that the danger has passed. When your heart rate slows and your muscles relax, the amygdala reduces its alarms, and the rational part of your brain can re-engage.

Fear also hijacks your perception, making threats feel bigger than they are. By changing your focus—shifting from "What if something bad happens?" to "What is actually happening right now?"—you can gently pull yourself out of the loop. This mental shift reduces the charge of fearful thoughts and helps reset the system without fighting it directly. Offering kindness to yourself during these moments reduces shame and builds resilience, making the panic loop less powerful the next time you feel it starting.

In summary, the panic loop is your brain and body's emergency survival system operating at full speed, even when no real emergency exists. It hijacks reasoning, amplifies physical symptoms, and traps you in cycles of fear. But understanding how it works gives you control. By learning to interrupt the loop quickly—whether through breath, body awareness, or simple shifts in thinking—you reclaim your calm and prevent anxiety from owning your moments. Knowing that you can stop this process anytime is the first step to breaking free and living with greater peace.

DR. AVA KINGSLEY, PSYD

THE 90-SECOND WINDOW: SCIENCE BEHIND THE METHOD

When anxiety flares, it often feels like the moment drags on forever. Yet, science reveals a surprising truth: your body's acute stress response, which fuels that surge of panic or worry, actually lasts only about 90 seconds. This brief but intense period—what we call the "90-second window"—is where your brain and body are most reactive and malleable. Understanding this window can change how you deal with anxiety, turning moments that once felt overwhelming into manageable experiences.

Your brain is wired to respond to threats quickly. When you sense danger, real or imagined, the amygdala—your brain's emotional alarm system—springs into action. It triggers the release of stress hormones like adrenaline and cortisol, preparing your body for "fight or flight." Heart rate spikes, breathing quickens, muscles tense up, and a flood of sensations sweeps through you. This intense physical and emotional reaction happens fast, often before your conscious mind even registers what's going on.

But here's what's crucial: this heightened state doesn't keep going endlessly if you don't feed it. After that initial burst, if you don't add fuel by continuing to panic or spiral into catastrophic thinking, the stress chemicals start to wash away. Your nervous system begins to calm down naturally, usually within 90 seconds. This means the panic or anxiety attack, no matter how intense it feels, is actually self-limiting at its core.

Why does this matter? Most people don't realize that their anxiety has a clear expiration timer if it's left alone or interrupted. Instead, the typical response is to resist or fight the feeling, which can ironically extend the experience or make it worse. The science behind the 90-second window shows that instead of battling anxiety as though it's endless, you can learn to recognize and work with this natural rhythm.

Think of this window as a critical moment of opportunity. When anxiety starts to spike, you've got roughly one and a half minutes to gently interrupt the cascade before it takes over your entire system. It's much easier—and more effective—to shift gears early on rather than waiting for panic to reach a crescendo. That's why the tools and techniques discussed in this book revolve around acting quickly, consistently, and intentionally in these first moments.

The nervous system is incredibly adaptable, but it's also sensitive to timing. If you engage your body and brain right after the initial flood of fear, you leverage a unique chance to recalibrate. The calming signals you send—whether through your breath, body, or focus—can redirect neural pathways and dampen the overactive alarm signal. This quick intervention prevents the brain from encoding the anxious moment as a bigger threat than it actually is, reducing the intensity of future episodes.

This process aligns with what researchers call "neuroplasticity," your brain's capacity to reorganize itself through experience. When you engage in specific behaviors within these 90 seconds, you can weaken the anxiety response pattern and strengthen calmer, more grounded neural circuits. Over time and with practice, these small changes add up, making anxiety less frequent and less severe.

Interestingly, the 90-second window is not just a theoretical concept—it's been backed by multiple studies on stress and emotional regulation. For example, physiological data shows that heart rate and cortisol spikes begin to drop after about a minute and a half if there's no sustained threat or ongoing anxiety response. Psychological experiments reveal that quick mindfulness or grounding practices performed in the first moments of anxiety significantly reduce panic symptoms.

Moreover, the window highlights why "waiting it out" often works, even if it feels impossible in the moment. The problem isn't that you can't handle anxiety—it's that your brain's natural defense system overshoots, and you end up caught in the fear spiral. Recognizing the 90-second limit transforms your perspective. You start to see anxiety as a passing wave rather than an all-consuming storm, and that shift alone can reduce its power.

At the biological level, the sympathetic nervous system (SNS), responsible for the fight-or-flight reaction, activates instantly when you detect danger. But the parasympathetic nervous system (PNS) works behind the scenes to calm things back down. The 90-second window corresponds to the time it takes the PNS to kick back in fully and bring your body toward balance again. Practices that help activate the PNS—like controlled breathing or grounding techniques—accelerate this calming phase.

One of the most empowering takeaways is that you don't have to be a passive victim to anxiety. You can become an active participant in redirecting your nervous system during these crucial moments. This science-based framework provides not just hope but practical control. When you understand the physiology and timing, you gain a roadmap out of panic rather than feeling lost in it.

It's also important to address why many anxiety sufferers feel like their symptoms last longer than 90 seconds. The difference is often in what happens after the initial rush. If your mind dwells on the feelings, catastrophizes, or tries desperately to suppress the anxiety, this cognitive activity can sustain or even amplify the stress response. The brain amplifies signals through rumination or "thought loops," keeping the discomfort alive well beyond that natural 90-second phase. This is where intentional interruption through quick, accessible methods makes a huge difference.

To contrast, think about a time when you felt a sudden jolt of fear—like nearly stepping into oncoming traffic or hearing a loud, unexpected noise. That spike in nervous system activity is shocking, but it typically fades fast if the threat disappears. The body's system resets quickly. Anxiety is the brain and body activating this same ancient alarm system, but often triggered by harmless thoughts or situations. Knowing the true length of this stress response helps reframe these feelings as temporary and manageable.

By aligning your responses with this 90-second biology, you essentially hack into your body's natural rhythm. Instead of reacting unconsciously, you engage consciously at the exact moment the brain is most primed for change. This explains why even brief, focused interventions can have outsized effects on your anxiety levels. It's about working smarter, not harder, with your mind and body's own mechanisms.

To sum up, the 90-second window isn't magic or guesswork—it's a scientifically grounded insight into how anxiety unfolds in your brain and body. Seeing anxiety through this lens taps into your brain's built-in reset function, giving you a realistic and rapid timeframe to regain control.

As you practice the techniques in upcoming chapters that leverage this window, you'll notice something remarkable: over time, your brain rewires itself to respond less frantically. The more consistently you respect this 90-second rhythm, the quicker you become at calming your system and preventing full-blown panic.

Remember, anxiety is a signal, not a permanent state. The 90-second window is your brain's natural breathing room. Whichever strategies you choose to employ, the goal is simple—to reclaim those precious seconds and use them to shift your experience from chaos to calm in an instant. Understanding the science behind these moments is the foundation for everything that follows, empowering you to take quick, confident action whenever anxiety tries to take hold.

DR. AVA KINGSLEY, PSYD

WHY YOU DON'T NEED TO "FIX" YOURSELF TO FEEL BETTER

It's easy to fall into the trap of thinking there's something inherently wrong with you when anxiety shows up. The way anxiety bombards your mind with "what ifs," self-doubt, or racing thoughts often feels like a personal failure or a glitch in your wiring. But here's the truth: you don't need to "fix" yourself to find relief or experience peace. Anxiety is not a broken part of you—it's part of how your brain reacts to stress, threat, or uncertainty. Recognizing this can change everything about how you relate to your experience of anxiety.

When anxiety flares, it feels urgent and overwhelming, making it tempting to want an immediate fix. Society often pushes the idea of fixing problems quickly, so when it comes to mental health, many assume they must overhaul their entire self to be "normal" or calm. But that's a misleading narrative. Anxiety isn't a personal defect that needs repair; it's a response system designed to keep you safe, albeit sometimes overzealous. Trying to "fix" yourself the way you might fix a broken gadget puts unnecessary pressure on you and can make anxiety feel like a personal flaw.

It's important to understand that anxiety isn't a character flaw or a sign of weakness. Instead, it's a signal, a reaction made by your nervous system trying to protect you from perceived danger. Sometimes, that danger isn't real or immediate, but your brain doesn't always make a distinction. Rather than needing to fix who you are, what you actually need is to learn new ways to respond to these signals—ways that let you manage anxiety without feeling overwhelmed or defined by it.

One of the biggest hurdles people face is the constant pressure to "be better" or "stop feeling this way." That pressure itself can fuel anxiety, creating a cycle where the more you try to fix yourself, the more stuck you feel. This cycle feeds the panic loop, where fear generates more fear, and suddenly, you're caught in a spiral of self-judgment and tension. Instead of breaking that cycle with self-criticism, it helps to take a gentler approach.

Think of yourself as a teammate rather than a project that needs fixing. The aim isn't to eliminate anxiety entirely—because that's unrealistic—but to build a working relationship with it. You don't have to be perfect, and you don't have to get rid of every anxious thought. What changes everything is how you respond to those thoughts and feelings the moment they arise.

Many people believe that if anxiety is present, it means something is seriously wrong, and this belief creates unnecessary shame. Shame can hide beneath anxiety, making it even harder to reach out or practice simple tools for relief. But shame isn't your friend here. It's simply a feeling that arises when your mind misunderstands anxiety as failure. Instead of trying to fix yourself, shift your focus to accepting anxiety as part of the human experience. Acceptance doesn't mean resignation or giving up; it means making space for anxiety without letting it control you.

Another misconception is that you have to completely overhaul your identity or personality to manage anxiety. That's just not true. You don't have to become someone else or change your essential self to feel better. Just like learning to ride a bike doesn't require rebuilding your entire body, managing anxiety involves learning new skills, practicing fresh habits, and rewiring the way your mind processes stressful moments. These small adjustments create big shifts in how you experience your life.

People often confuse "fixing" anxiety with "curing" it overnight. It's natural to want drastic solutions, but sustainable change happens step by step, with consistent practice. The tools and techniques you'll discover throughout this book aren't about changing who you are; they're about empowering you to calm the nervous system and shift your brain's reactions in real time. These tools fit into your existing life—they don't require a complete transformation of your identity or beliefs.

Remember this: anxiety is part of your story, but it's not the whole story. When you stop trying to fix yourself, you begin the journey toward self-compassion and understanding. You start to see anxiety as a visitor rather than a permanent resident. This mindset shift is powerful—it reduces resistance and encourages curiosity, making tools and practices more effective because you're working with your brain, not against it.

Many folks fall into the trap of wondering why they "shouldn't" feel anxious—that it's irrational or something a strong person wouldn't experience. While challenging some anxious thoughts can be helpful, it's equally important to acknowledge that anxiety is a very natural reaction. Accepting that you don't need to change your core essence to feel better lets you approach anxiety without self-judgment, which is often the fuel that keeps panic fires burning.

Rather than building walls to keep anxiety out, you'll learn how to open doors to understanding it. This shift lets you reclaim control by choosing how you engage with anxious thoughts and feelings. It's less about "fixing" yourself and more about retraining your brain to behave differently under pressure. The brain's remarkable ability to change, known as neuroplasticity, is your ally, and you don't need to wait for a crisis to start rewiring those pathways.

It's also worth acknowledging how helpful it is to change your internal dialogue from "What's wrong with me?" to "What's happening to me right now?" This small language shift reduces blame and provides a clearer, more manageable perspective on anxiety. It's okay to feel anxious. You're not broken, defective, or flawed just because anxiety shows up. Instead, you're navigating a common human experience—and you have access to quick, effective techniques that work with your brain's design.

DR. AVA KINGSLEY, PSYD

In a culture that often emphasizes being fixed or perfect, embracing the idea that you don't need to fix yourself to feel better can feel revolutionary. It frees you to focus on growth and healing without the crushing weight of self-criticism. It invites patience and kindness, both crucial for sustained progress.

Most importantly, this perspective encourages you to trust the process. Change is happening even if it feels slow or invisible. The goal isn't perfection—it's progress. Anxiety may visit again, but with every new tool you build and each practice you engage in, you're reclaiming your power over it. You move from feeling trapped by anxiety to mastering moments in which anxiety appears.

So as you move forward, remember: you're not broken and you don't need to be fixed. Instead, you're learning to navigate anxiety with skill, acceptance, and increasing confidence. This approach sets the foundation for relief that's not just temporary but lasting, helping you live fully even when anxiety arises.

Chapter 2
The 90-Second Tools for Instant Relief

When anxiety hits, the hardest part is often just getting a grip on the moment before it spirals out of control, and that's where the 90-second tools come into play—they're designed to interrupt the panic fast, right when it starts. These strategies tap into simple, accessible actions like focusing your senses, controlling your breath, or shifting your thoughts to calm your nervous system and stop the flood of fear in its tracks. You don't need fancy equipment or hours of meditation; all it takes is a minute and a half to start rewiring your brain's reaction and reclaim a sense of calm. This chapter will introduce you to practical, science-backed techniques that anyone can use anytime, anywhere to break free from the overwhelming grip of anxiety and move toward feeling grounded again.

DR. AVA KINGSLEY, PSYD

TOOL 1: GROUNDING IN THE MOMENT (THE 5-4-3-2-1 RESET)

When anxiety hits hard, the world can start to feel like it's spinning out of control. Your mind races, your heart pounds, and every thought seems louder than the last. This is where grounding techniques like the 5-4-3-2-1 reset come in—simple, swift tools that can pull you out of the chaos and back into the present moment. This tool doesn't rely on fancy equipment or long practice sessions. It's straightforward, effective, and—most importantly—you can use it anytime, anywhere. Whether you're stuck in traffic, sitting at your desk, or lying awake in the middle of the night, the 5-4-3-2-1 reset can help you regain control in 90 seconds or less.

The idea behind grounding is to anchor your awareness firmly in the "here and now." Anxiety often makes us feel disconnected—from reality, from our bodies, and from what's actually happening around us. The 5-4-3-2-1 reset works by guiding your attention through your five senses, one step at a time. This multisensory approach interrupts the spiral of frightening thoughts and physical symptoms that anxiety tends to amplify.

Here's how it works: identify 5 things you can see around you, 4 things you can feel (physical sensations), 3 things you can hear, 2 things you can smell, and 1 thing you can taste. These simple actions might seem almost childlike, but their power lies in how they shift your brain's focus outward, dialing down the internal alarm system. What's fascinating is that this method is backed by neurological research—it activates the prefrontal cortex, the area of the brain responsible for reasoning and decision-making, which can help calm the amygdala, the part driving your fight-or-flight response during panic.

As you begin to name and recognize each thing with all your senses, your brain starts to reconnect with the present, slowing down the flood of worries and tension. You're not trying to "push away" your anxiety; instead, you're inviting your brain to engage in a different, more grounded reality. The beauty of the 5-4-3-2-1 reset is that it doesn't demand more energy from you; it simply redirects existing energy in a way that feels tangible and manageable.

Let's break down each step in a bit more detail, so you feel confident using this tool whenever you need it. Start with your eyes and look around. Find five things you can see right now. It doesn't matter what they are—a clock on the wall, a plant on a windowsill, your own hand resting on your lap. Naming these items aloud or mentally helps your brain shift from internal chaos to external observation.

Next, touch four things around you. This could be the texture of your clothing, the smooth surface of a table, the coolness of your water bottle, or the sensation of your feet planted on the floor. Physical sensations are a powerful way to keep your mind from racing because they're concrete, immediate, and impossible to ignore.

Then, listen carefully and notice three different sounds. Maybe it's the hum of air conditioning, the chirping of birds outside, or the distant murmur of conversation. Hearing without judgment, simply observing, helps you stay rooted where you are.

After that, bring your attention to your sense of smell and identify two scents. If you're in an environment without obvious smells, try to access a familiar one—like the scent of fresh coffee in your mind or the fragrance of soap on your hands. Engaging this sense might feel tricky at first, but with practice, it becomes easier and quite calming.

Finally, note one thing you can taste. Maybe it's the lingering flavor of toothpaste or a sip of water. Focusing here rounds out the sensory experience and gently signals your brain that this moment, right here, is safe and within your control.

One thing to remember is that the 5-4-3-2-1 reset doesn't need to be perfect. If you struggle to find smells or tastes at first, just do your best and move on. The goal isn't to tick every box flawlessly but to create a flow of awareness that pulls you away from panic. Over time, this process builds what many call a "grounding muscle," strengthening your ability to self-soothe during stressful moments.

This tool is especially powerful because it's both immediate and accessible. You don't have to sit down and meditate for half an hour or wait for anxiety to pass on its own. The 5-4-3-2-1 reset gives you a quick, reliable way to interrupt anxiety as it starts, turning an overwhelming wave into manageable moments.

Using this technique regularly helps retrain your brain's automatic responses. Instead of spiraling into dread or helplessness, your nervous system learns to pause and reconnect with reality. This rewiring is key for long-term anxiety reduction—but the instant relief this tool offers is what makes it a go-to in crisis moments.

People often ask if they can use this method anywhere, and the answer is a resounding yes. One of its biggest advantages is how unobtrusive it is. You can do it quietly while sitting in a meeting, standing in line, or even walking through a busy grocery store. It doesn't require special equipment or space; your senses and your presence are all you need.

If you're just starting or feel overwhelmed, try pairing the 5-4-3-2-1 reset with deep, slow breaths. This combination can maximize the calming effect by reducing your body's fight-or-flight tension while your mind reconnects with the present. But even on its own, this tool can break the cycle of anxiety and panic, one sense at a time.

Working through this reset also nurtures a powerful shift in how you relate to anxiety. Rather than feeling controlled by it, you're beginning to take ownership of your experience and response. Each time you anchor in the moment, you assert that anxiety does not have to dictate your day.

In addition to being practical, the 5-4-3-2-1 reset can be surprisingly empowering. Anxiety can make you feel small and out of control—but this simple practice reminds you that your brain and body have built-in switches to regain calm. Using this technique regularly builds confidence and resilience. You start to believe that you really do have tools to navigate anxiety, even when it feels overwhelming.

One of the secrets to successful grounding is practice. Like any skill, the more you use the 5-4-3-2-1 reset, the quicker and easier it becomes. Integrate it into your daily routine—not just in moments of anxiety but anytime you need a mental pause. It can anchor you in stressful situations before panic takes hold, and over time, reduce the frequency and intensity of anxious episodes.

Remember, the goal here isn't to eliminate anxiety completely; that's unrealistic and unnecessary. Instead, this tool teaches you how to step off the escalator of panic, slow your heart, and approach each moment with a clearer and calmer mind. In doing so, it's possible to reclaim your focus, your composure, and ultimately, your sense of peace.

The 5-4-3-2-1 reset is much more than a checklist—it's a doorway to mindfulness in disguise. No matter how intense your anxiety feels right now, grounding yourself through sensory awareness is an accessible, compassionate way to reclaim control. The best part? It only takes 90 seconds, but those seconds can feel like a breath of fresh air in the middle of a storm.

TOOL 2: TACTICAL BREATHING (CALM IN 60 SECONDS)

When anxiety hits, the rapid heartbeat, shallow breathing, and tight chest can feel overwhelming. Your body's response to stress kicks into overdrive, flooding you with adrenaline that leaves you feeling out of control. Tactical breathing is a powerful way to counter that flood and reclaim calm within just 60 seconds. It's a simple yet effective method designed to regulate your breathing, calm your nervous system, and interrupt the panic spiral before it grows. Using tactical breathing in those moments of high anxiety can make you feel grounded, centered, and back in the driver's seat of your own mind.

At its core, tactical breathing is about slowing down your breath and controlling its rhythm. While it may sound basic, focusing on your breath this way changes the chemistry inside your body. It reduces the fight-or-flight response by activating the parasympathetic nervous system—that's the branch of your nervous system responsible for rest and digestion. In other words, tactical breathing tells your brain that you're safe, allowing your heart rate to slow and your mind to switch out of panic mode. That shift happens quickly, which is why the method works so well as a go-to 90-second tool.

The key to tactical breathing lies in a precise pattern: inhale deeply for a count of four, hold your breath for four counts, exhale slowly for four, and then pause for four counts before repeating. This 4-4-4-4 rhythm is sometimes called "box breathing" or "square breathing." You can try it anywhere—on a stressful phone call, in traffic, or even during a triggering social situation. It requires no props or special setting, which makes it accessible for any moment you need fast relief.

Don't underestimate the power of just paying attention to your breath. When anxiety takes hold, your breathing often becomes shallow and erratic. This restricts oxygen flow, which actually makes anxiety worse. Deliberate tactical breathing breaks that cycle by increasing oxygen to your brain and calming your body. It helps interrupt the panic loop that fuels many anxiety attacks. Within a minute, you can feel your pulse slow, your muscles release tension, and your mind become clearer.

Learning tactical breathing is like having a reset button for your nervous system. Once the pattern is familiar, you can call on it instantly whenever stress arises. This skill becomes an immediate anchor to pull you away from overwhelming adrenaline and back into your present moment. Many people who suffer from anxiety or panic attacks find it useful to practice tactical breathing regularly, even when they're not anxious. That way, the technique becomes second nature, ready to be used clearly and confidently when anxiety strikes.

It's worth noting that mastering this method doesn't mean forcing your breath or holding it too long. The goal is to find a comfortable but deliberate rhythm that soothes rather than strains. If four counts feel too long, you can start with three and gradually work up as you get more comfortable. The important part is keeping the breathing controlled and consistent, which sends calming signals to your brain.

Here's how to get started with tactical breathing step-by-step:

1. **Find a quiet spot if you can.** Sit or stand comfortably with your back straight but relaxed.
2. **Close your eyes if it feels safe.** If not, simply soften your gaze.
3. **Begin with a deep inhale.** Breathe in slowly and smoothly through your nose to the count of four.
4. **Hold the breath gently.** Count to four without straining or clenching your body.
5. **Exhale slowly through your mouth or nose.** Aim for a smooth, controlled breath out lasting four seconds.
6. **Pause and hold empty lungs.** Count four again before starting the next inhale.
7. **Repeat this cycle.** Continue for several rounds until you notice your heart rate slowing and your mind clearing.

Because this breathing technique targets both your body and mind simultaneously, it fits perfectly within the 90-second framework. With practice, you can complete four or five full cycles in about a minute, enough to make a real difference in your anxiety level. Veterans of tactical breathing often report that even a single cycle can provide a noticeable reduction in immediate panic symptoms.

A crucial element that sets tactical breathing apart from just "taking deep breaths" is its intentional pacing. Rapid deep breaths without control can trigger dizziness or hyperventilation, worsening anxiety symptoms. The steady tempo and balanced inhaling and exhaling protect you from this, keeping you grounded. It also empowers you because you're actively doing something to influence your state instead of feeling helpless.

The science behind tactical breathing backs up its effectiveness. Research shows that modulating breath this way impacts the autonomic nervous system by improving heart rate variability (HRV). Higher HRV is linked to better stress resilience and emotional regulation. Simply put, tactical breathing can make your body more efficient at bouncing back from stress over time. This means using this technique regularly could potentially improve not just momentary relief but your long-term mental health.

Another benefit is how tactical breathing engages your focus. When you direct your attention to the counts and rhythm, it gently pulls you out of negative thought cycles common in anxiety attacks. This redirection, paired with the physical effects on your nervous system, creates a powerful one-two punch to panic. And because it requires nothing but your breath, you can practice tactical breathing discreetly anywhere—no one even needs to know you're doing it.

STOP ANXIETY NOW

For many people, the idea of slowing their breath during anxiety can feel counterintuitive at first. When panic flares, your instinct might be to breathe faster or gulp for air. But tactical breathing teaches you to breathe with intention, which brings relief and control instead of chaos. It's a skill that, once learned, can transform overwhelming moments into manageable ones.

As you incorporate tactical breathing into your toolkit, remember it's not about perfection. You don't have to "get it right" every time, nor make every breath exactly four seconds long. The practice itself is the medicine. Even an imperfect attempt can calm your nervous system and shift your mindset.

Some people find it helpful to pair tactical breathing with a quiet mental phrase or affirmation, like "calm" or "steady." This layered focus heightens the relaxation response. Others prefer simply to concentrate on the breath counts and sensations in their chest or belly. Experiment to find what works best for you. One of the biggest advantages of tactical breathing is its flexibility.

Consider making tactical breathing a habit outside of stressful moments too. Set aside a few minutes daily just to practice the pattern when you're calm and relaxed. Over time, your nervous system will start to tune in to this rhythm as a signal to relax. This helps build resilience so that anxiety struggles less to throw you off balance.

In intense situations, tactical breathing serves as a lifeline. Instead of feeling trapped by racing thoughts and a pounding heart, you hold something concrete—your breath. This method puts the power back in your hands. It reminds you that even while anxiety tries to hijack your experience, you can take immediate action to calm your mind and body.

In summary, tactical breathing is one of the most accessible, science-backed ways to quiet your anxiety within 60 seconds. By mastering this controlled breathing pattern, you can learn to pause panic before it spirals. It doesn't require time, money, or special equipment—just your attention and a little practice. Built into your daily rhythm, tactical breathing becomes a reliable skill that guides you through turbulent emotional seas, restoring calm and clarity in the blink of an eye.

TOOL 3: INSTANT REFRAME (SHIFT THE THOUGHT SPIRAL)

When anxiety kicks in, your mind often gets caught in a rapid-fire spiral of negative thoughts. It feels like a runaway train you can't stop, where one worry leads to another, and suddenly it's overwhelming. That's where the Instant Reframe tool comes in. It's designed to disrupt that spiraling pattern fast—within 90 seconds—so you can take back control of your thoughts before they snowball into a full-blown panic attack.

The core idea behind Instant Reframe is simple: you shift the way you interpret what's happening in your mind. Instead of accepting those automatic anxious thoughts as facts, you learn to see them as just thoughts—fleeting mental events that don't have to define your reality. This shift might sound straightforward, but it's incredibly powerful. It's about training your brain to pause and challenge its first reaction, replacing fear or judgment with a different perspective.

Think of your anxious thoughts like an echo chamber playing on repeat. The Instant Reframe tool helps you open the door to fresh air and a new soundtrack. By stepping back and changing the narrative, you take the energy out of the negative loop. This doesn't mean ignoring what you feel or pretending everything is fine. Instead, you're actively choosing to respond differently. You're inviting curiosity and calm where there was once only worry.

DR. AVA KINGSLEY, PSYD

How do you actually do this? The first step is to catch yourself in the moment the anxious thoughts arise. This is where the 90-second window matters—once you're past that, your brain has usually locked deeper into stress. Quickly recognize the thought that's fueling your anxiety, then intentionally reframe it. For example, if your mind screams "I'm going to fail," reframe it to, "This is a tough moment, but I've handled hard things before." Or change "I can't handle this" to "I'm doing the best I can right now."

These changes in thought aren't about naïve positivity or sugarcoating reality. They're about shifting your perspective enough to break the grip anxiety has on your mind. By doing this practice repeatedly, it becomes easier and more natural to pause the panic spiral before it consumes you. The Instant Reframe tool trains your brain to spot distorted thinking patterns—like catastrophizing or black-and-white thinking—and swap them with a balanced, compassionate view.

One helpful way to get started is to create your own "go-to" reframes. These are simple, realistic statements that resonate with you personally—phrases that ground you and offer a moment of relief when anxiety flares. Write them down or memorize them so they're ready when you need them. You might find it helpful to think of these reframes as mental safety nets, catching you as you fall into that anxious pit.

It's also key to be gentle with yourself during this process. Instant Reframing isn't about forcing your thoughts to "just stop" or berating yourself for feeling anxious. Anxiety is a natural response, and the goal here is to meet yourself with kindness while steering your mind toward less distressing places. Over time, this practice changes how your brain expects challenges to unfold, which reduces the overall intensity and frequency of anxious episodes.

Instant Reframe is accessible because it requires no special equipment, doesn't take a lot of time, and can be done anywhere—even on a crowded bus or in the middle of a stressful meeting. Because it works on the cognitive level, it complements other tools that target the body, like breathing or grounding. When you combine these strategies, you'll find relief coming faster and sticking longer.

One common hesitation people have when trying to reframe their anxiety is that it feels like suppressing or denying what's really there. But think of reframing as looking through a different lens, not erasing your experience. You're not invalidating how you feel—you're giving your mind permission to see the situation from another angle, one that isn't so reactive or heavy. This new viewpoint offers breathing room and subtle control over your emotional state.

Another important element is consistency. This tool is designed for those quick moments when anxiety starts to ramp up, but its true power unfolds when you practice it regularly, even when you're feeling calm. Training your brain to find balance early on builds resilience and rewires neural pathways over time. You're actively rewiring the anxiety loop into a new pattern of thoughtful, compassionate response.

To sum it up: Instant Reframe works because it interrupts the anxiety spiral by rewriting the story your mind is telling itself. By catching negative thoughts early and shifting them to a more balanced viewpoint, you weaken the panic response and regain mental clarity. This tool empowers you to be an active participant in managing your anxiety, rather than a passenger overwhelmed by it.

Give yourself permission to experiment with different reframes and find what truly helps you feel steadier. Change might not happen overnight, but with every use of Instant Reframe, you're shaping a calmer mindset and reclaiming your peace.

TOOL 4: TENSE AND RELEASE (BODY-BASED RELIEF)

When anxiety hits hard, the rush of tension in your body can feel overwhelming—tight muscles, rapid heartbeat, shallow breathing. Sometimes, your mind races so fast that calming your thoughts seems impossible. That's exactly why Tool 4, Tense and Release, is such a powerful addition to your toolkit. This technique, rooted in simple body awareness and physical relief, helps you cut through the neurological chaos in just 90 seconds by focusing on muscle tension and letting it go.

The science behind this tool is straightforward but impressive. During anxiety or panic, your sympathetic nervous system kicks into high gear, producing that "fight or flight" response that tenses your muscles and jars your system out of balance. Tense and Release works by deliberately contracting your muscles, holding that tension momentarily, and then fully releasing it, which sends calming signals back to your nervous system. This switch essentially flips a physical "off" switch to the stress response, pulling you out of the spiral and into a more grounded, relaxed state.

One of the biggest benefits? It's accessible anywhere and anytime. You don't need special equipment or a quiet room. Whether you're sitting at your desk, standing in line, or lying in bed, you can plug into your body and release tension right there. This makes it perfect for those sudden moments when anxiety flares unpredictably.

To start with Tense and Release, pick a muscle group you can easily engage—your hands, shoulders, or legs work well. Clench or tighten those muscles as firmly as feels safe, aiming for about five to ten seconds. It's important here not to push yourself into pain; you want a good tension that's noticeable but comfortable. After holding the tension steadily, completely release it, letting go with intention. Notice how the muscles suddenly feel softer, looser, perhaps even a little warmer. That contrast between tension and release is the core of the technique's calming effect.

Many people report feeling an almost immediate sense of spaciousness in their bodies after doing this, which reflects the nervous system moving out of hyperarousal. What's striking is how this quick physical reset can also bring mental relief. When your body stops screaming in tension, your mind often quiets down, breaking that endless loop of worry and fear that fuels anxiety.

You can cycle through multiple muscle groups to deepen the effect. For instance, after your hands, try your shoulders, neck, or even your feet and calves. Spend 30 seconds to a minute doing this whole-body check: tense, hold, release, and observe. Breaking the physical tension can be surprisingly grounding—or as some say, like a mini-body reboot.

STOP ANXIETY NOW

For those who struggle with chronic tension or who experience panic attacks regularly, practicing Tense and Release daily can create a valuable habit. The more your nervous system learns to "let go," the easier it becomes to catch yourself early in anxious moments and give yourself relief before panic escalates. It's like training a muscle—your ability to calm your body strengthens with consistent practice.

This tool also ties into the mind-body connection, a crucial concept in managing anxiety. Anxiety is often thought of as purely a mental issue, but in reality, your body experiences it just as much, if not more. By addressing tension physically, Tense and Release bridges the gap between mind and body, helping to "ground" you in the present moment. This grounding prevents the "what-ifs" and racing thoughts that amplify anxiety from spiraling out of control.

Another powerful part of this technique is its simplicity. During intense anxiety, complicated methods or cognitive exercises might feel out of reach. Your brain searches for immediate relief. Tense and Release offers a quick, tactile action you can do without overthinking. It bypasses the need to "fix" your thoughts right away and instead offers physical relief that leads to mental calm.

To make the most of this technique, pairing it with slow, deep breaths boosts effectiveness. After releasing the tension, inhale deeply through your nose and exhale gently through your mouth. This breathing rhythm informs your brain that the threat isn't immediate, reinforcing the relaxation response initiated through muscle release.

There's also a psychological aspect here worth noting. When anxiety spikes, your mind often tells you that you're "weak" or "out of control." Practicing Tense and Release reframes this story because it's an active step you're taking. By physically engaging your body, you're demonstrating control, resilience, and self-care. This can be incredibly empowering and help rebuild confidence with every session.

Some anxiety sufferers find Tense and Release works well as a preventive practice too. Before going into potentially stressful situations—like a social event, presentation, or even a daily commute—they do a brief session to "check in" with their body. This proactive approach can reduce baseline tension, making those events feel less triggering.

It's important to be patient with yourself while learning this tool. At first, it might feel awkward to deliberately tense muscles or focus on releasing tension in a conscious way. Don't let perfectionism get in your head. Like any new skill, it takes time. Even small, imperfect attempts bring benefits and build familiarity. Over time, the muscle memory develops, and your nervous system remembers how to "turn off" anxiety more quickly.

Lastly, this tool enhances emotional regulation beyond anxiety. Stress, anger, frustration—all these emotions create physical tension. Tense and Release helps you notice these sensations sooner and cultivate calm, even in intense moments. It's a versatile strategy that serves your overall mental health.

In practice, consider setting reminders to check in with your body a few times a day. Use pauses during work or breaks to do quick rounds of Tense and Release. You might notice how your body shifts from tightness to relaxation, drawing your attention away from anxious thoughts and back into the here and now. Over days and weeks, this helps create a sense of safety inside your own body—a foundation for lasting change.

In summary, Tool 4: Tense and Release taps into your body's natural ability to calm itself through a simple physical ritual. By intentionally squeezing and then letting go, you interrupt the stress cycle and signal to your nervous system that it's safe to relax. This technique doesn't just ease muscle tightness; it rewires how you respond to anxiety on a deep level. And because it's quick, easy, and portable, it's one of the best 90-second tools for instant relief you can rely on anywhere, anytime.

DR. AVA KINGSLEY, PSYD

TOOL 5: THE COLD RESET (ACTIVATE YOUR VAGUS NERVE)

When anxiety strikes, it often feels like your nervous system is out of control—as if your body is primed for danger even when there's no real threat. One of the fastest ways to interrupt this overwhelming surge is by activating your vagus nerve through a simple—but powerful—cold reset technique. This method taps into your body's built-in calming system, helping to turn down the dial on stress and bring you back to a place of balance quickly.

The vagus nerve is the longest cranial nerve in your body, winding down from your brain through your neck and chest into your abdomen. It plays a crucial role in regulating your parasympathetic nervous system, which is responsible for slowing your heart rate, promoting digestion, and calming your breath. When anxiety flares up, often your sympathetic nervous system—the "fight or flight" part—has taken the wheel. The cold reset reminds your body it's safe by stimulating the vagus nerve, signaling that it's time to relax.

This tool is deceptively simple. It involves exposing your face or neck to a blast of cold, like holding a cold pack, splashing cold water on your face, or simply placing a cold, damp washcloth on your cheeks or eyes. These cold sensations trigger the dive reflex, an evolutionary response that slows your heart rate and lowers blood pressure, essentially forcing your body into a calmer, more regulated state. Even a brief

30 to 60 seconds of cold exposure can make a noticeable difference, especially if you use it consistently whenever you feel panic starting to build.

The beauty of the cold reset is that it's portable and requires no equipment beyond something cold you can find easily—a sink, a cold drink from the fridge, or even a bag of frozen peas in a pinch. This accessibility means you can use it anywhere: at home, at work, standing in line, or even in public without drawing attention. It lets you take control of your anxiety on your own terms, giving you a tool to interrupt the panic spiral immediately.

Start by grounding yourself in the moment before you apply the cold. This means a quick check-in: where are you feeling tension? Is your breath rapid? Your heart racing? Acknowledge these sensations without judgment—they're simply signals from your body that something is amped up. Then, take a slow, deep breath to prepare. Next, bring cold either from water or an ice pack up to your face, concentrating on the areas around your eyes and on your cheeks. Hold it there for about 30 seconds or longer, depending on what feels comfortable. You should notice a shift almost immediately—your breathing may slow, and a sense of calm can start seeping in.

Why does your body respond so quickly to cold on the face? It connects to that dive reflex mentioned earlier. When mammals' faces come into contact with cold water, it triggers a naturally calming physiological response. This reflex slows the heart rate to conserve oxygen during submersion—a trait once essential for survival in water. Humans have retained this reflex, and it's a wonderful shortcut to tapping into your nervous system's "off switch" when anxiety feels unbearable.

Some people find it helpful to combine the cold reset with tactical breathing (covered earlier) or grounding techniques to amplify relief. For example, try breathing slowly and deeply during the cold exposure, inhaling through your nose and exhaling gently through your mouth. This combo enhances parasympathetic activation, slowing your heart and quieting your mind. But if breathing feels overwhelming in the moment, just focus on the cold first. Let the sensation guide you back to a calmer state.

Besides being effective, the cold reset also empowers you with a sense of agency. Anxiety often makes you feel helpless and out of control, but placing a cold stimulus on your face is an action you can take immediately to arrest escalating panic. That small, intentional act helps your brain realize you're not at the mercy of your anxiety—it's a choice you make. This mindset shift can be incredibly liberating.

For those new to this tool, consistency and practice are essential. If you only use the cold reset during intense panic attacks, you might find it harder to harness the technique calmly under pressure. Instead, make it a part of your daily toolkit by trying it during milder moments of stress or even in a neutral state. The more familiar your nervous system becomes with this signal to relax, the more responsive and effective it will be when you truly need it.

It's also worth noting that the cold reset can be adapted to your personal preferences and environment. Some prefer splashing cold water on their face, while others prefer holding an ice cube gently on their cheek or the back of their neck. Experiment with different methods to discover what feels most soothing and effective for you. You might even find a certain timing rhythm or pattern that works best—such as several short cold exposures spaced over a couple of minutes rather than one continuous plunge.

While rare, if you have certain medical conditions—like cold agglutinin disease or severe respiratory issues—it's smart to check with your healthcare provider before regularly using cold stimuli. For most people, though, this tool is safe, non-invasive, and completely accessible.

In moments when anxiety tries to hijack your brain, the cold reset offers a scientifically proven way to reclaim control rapidly. It's like hitting a mental "refresh" button in under 90 seconds. When you feel your heart pounding or your thoughts spiraling, try this quick, intentional cold break. With consistent use, not only can it help you in the moment, but it also retrains your nervous system over time to respond to stress with greater resilience.

Remember, this tool isn't about "fixing" or eliminating anxiety entirely—that's a longer journey we'll explore later. Instead, the cold reset is about giving you immediate, actionable relief when it matters most. It's a step toward feeling less overwhelmed and more grounded in your own body, even when panic feels like it's taking over.

Incorporate the cold reset into your practice, and make it a trusted ally in your anxiety toolkit. Over time, you'll find that your nervous system learns to shift gears more smoothly, and you'll reclaim more moments of calm amidst the chaos. Use this tool not just as a rescue but as a regular reset, and watch your confidence in managing anxiety grow every day.

TOOL 6: "WHAT IF" TO "WHAT IS" (STOP FUTURE TRIPPING)

One of the biggest traps anxiety sets for us is the endless loop of "what if" scenarios. Those sinking feelings start when your mind jumps ahead, imagining all the worst possible outcomes of a situation that hasn't even happened yet. That mental drama is exhausting—and, honestly, mostly unhelpful. The sixth tool in our 90-second toolbox is all about shifting your focus from "what if" fears to "what is" realities. It's a fast way to snap yourself out of future tripping and bring your attention back to the moment at hand, right where you actually have control.

When you first feel the mental tug of "what if," it may feel automatic, like your brain is wired to run through a highlight reel of everything that could go wrong. Anxiety loves to mess with your sense of safety by painting grim pictures. That's why this tool works: it interrupts the pattern and pulls your focus away from imagined futures to the facts in front of you.

Start by noticing when your thoughts tip into "what if" territory. Maybe you catch yourself worrying about an upcoming social event, replaying every awkward thing you think you might say or how others might judge you. Or perhaps it's about health, finances, or work—those "what if I fail" or "what if this goes badly" stories we tell ourselves out loud or silently. Recognizing the pattern is the first step. You can't redirect your mind if you don't know where it's heading.

Once you're aware, gently pause and ask yourself, "What is actually happening right now?" Don't brush this off as a silly or simple question; it's the crux of the tool. Shift your mental focus from hypothetical disasters to present-moment facts. You might say something in your head like, "Right now, I am sitting here, breathing, and no harm has come to me." Or, "At this moment, the situation is calm, and I haven't experienced that worst-case scenario." The point isn't to deny your feelings but to ground yourself in what's real instead of what might be.

This can feel almost like a quick mental jolt—like unplugging your brain from a runaway train and planting it firmly back on solid ground. You're affirming the truth as you see it, without adding layers of imagined fear. Over time, practicing this shift helps weaken anxiety's grip and builds resilience to those persistent "what if" thought patterns.

It's important to approach this tool with both kindness and curiosity. Anxiety's "what if" questions often feel urgent and overwhelming, so don't expect the thoughts to vanish instantly. You're not trying to bully your mind into submission here. Instead, think of this as a quiet resetting — a way to tell yourself, "I'm right here. And I'm okay." That simple acknowledgement can be surprisingly powerful.

Here's an example: imagine you're starting to feel the pull of "What if I say something stupid at this meeting?"

STOP ANXIETY NOW

Instead of spiraling from there, stop and ask yourself, "What is happening right now?" Are you actually in the meeting? If not, where are you? Maybe you're safe at home or on your way there. Is there any immediate evidence that you've said something awkward—in this moment, no. This shift calms your nervous system by redirecting attention to the known and the true, which your brain interprets as safer.

If you want to take it a step further, you can even phrase it like, "I'm not in the meeting yet, and right now, I have the power to prepare myself." This can help transform vague fear into actionable steps. Maybe you remind yourself that you can practice what you want to say later or visualize a positive outcome instead. Focusing on "what is" creates space for hope and practical action rather than getting stuck in "what if" doom loops.

Sometimes, when anxiety gets really intense, it feels like no amount of rational thinking can break through. That's natural. Our brains didn't evolve to handle abstract and distant threats easily—they want immediate problems solved. But even then, pausing for a moment and centering yourself in the present helps reduce the flood of adrenaline racing through your body. You can even combine this tool with others we've covered, like tactical breathing or grounding, to calm your physical state at the same time.

There's also power in reframing the meaning behind your worries. "What if" questions often come with a negative story attached: "What if I mess up? That means I'm a failure."

When you pivot to "what is," you strip away the exaggeration and face the facts. You might find that "what is" actually paints a less threatening picture. If you practice this regularly, you teach your mind that uncertainty isn't as dangerous as it seemed. In fact, it becomes a signal to use your tools to stay calm and present.

Another benefit of this tool is how it combats the tendency to catastrophize—the habit of assuming the worst possible outcome will happen. That's a big driver of anxiety and panic. By focusing on the reality of "what is," you interrupt catastrophizing in its tracks. You acknowledge your fear but don't fuel it with imagined disasters. This can reduce the intensity of anxious moments and keep future worries from overwhelming you.

Remember, changing your thought patterns isn't about forcing your brain into a rigid "positive thinking" mode; it's about cultivating awareness and choice. When you catch a "what if" in your mind, it's a chance to decide where your attention goes. You can let anxiety lead you down a rabbit hole—or choose to return to the present with a grounded sense of reality.

The more often you practice this, the quicker your brain learns. After some repetition, you'll notice that even a flash of "what if" can be slowed, examined, and redirected before it snowballs into full-blown panic. That alone makes this 90-second tool invaluable because it fits right into your daily life. Anytime you sense future tripping creeping in, you can use the "what if" to "what is" switch as a mental reset.

It's also worth mentioning that emotion and logic don't always align easily when anxiety runs high. That's okay. Emotional brain areas tend to dominate during anxious moments, making reasoned thinking feel out of reach. Returning to "what is" isn't about intellectual debate—it's about reconnecting with the present experience in a simple, direct way. Sometimes, just stating facts out loud or silently can bypass overwhelming feelings enough to create some breathing room.

This tool works well aside from big anxiety attacks too. It's useful whenever you notice stress creeping into your mind about stuff that hasn't happened yet—like upcoming deadlines, conversations, or health worries. If left unchecked, "what if" thoughts can drain your energy all day long. Practicing "what is" breaks that cycle and helps you reclaim mental space for things that truly matter.

In summary, "What If" to "What Is" is a deceptively simple but highly effective 90-second tool to halt future tripping. It's about shifting your mental attention away from imagined problems toward present realities. By doing so, you calm your nervous system, reduce catastrophic thinking, and reclaim control over your mind. Over time, this practice reprograms your anxiety brain to respond with clarity instead of chaos.

DR. AVA KINGSLEY, PSYD

This isn't about denying or ignoring your fears—it's about seeing them for what they really are: stories your mind is telling, not facts to live by. Developing this habit makes a huge difference in how you experience anxiety day to day, and it's a skill you can pull out anytime, anywhere. The next time your brain presses "play" on those "what if" fears, try shifting your focus to "what is" and see how quickly your sense of calm follows.

TOOL 7: THE 90-SECOND JOURNAL (TRACK AND TRAIN YOUR BRAIN)

When anxiety takes hold, it's easy to feel like your mind is out of control. Thoughts spiral, emotions surge, and you can lose track of what's real and what's fear playing tricks on you. That's why **The 90-Second Journal** is such a powerful tool—it helps you catch those feelings and thoughts as they happen and gently retrains your brain to respond differently. This tool doesn't require hours of writing or deep analysis. Instead, it's designed to fit in the cracks of your day, making it accessible even when anxiety is high and time feels scarce.

At its core, the 90-Second Journal is about quick, focused reflection. It asks you to pause and jot down a few key things—usually your current emotional state, a brief description of what triggered you, and a quick note on how you responded or want to respond differently next time. This simple exercise bridges awareness and action, helping you notice patterns without getting lost in overwhelm.

Why 90 seconds? Research shows that brief, deliberate moments of reflection are enough to activate the brain's prefrontal cortex, the area responsible for rational thinking and emotional regulation. When anxiety strikes, the amygdala—the brain's alarm system—can hijack your thoughts and body. But by stopping to track your experience right away for just a minute and a half, you create a tiny but powerful interruption in that cycle. It's enough time to shift gears mentally without feeling burdensome.

Think of the journal as a mini mental tune-up. Each entry rewires your brain a little bit, strengthening your ability to observe without reacting impulsively. Over days and weeks, these 90-second snapshots build a map of your anxiety triggers and responses. That map becomes your guide, helping you see where you're stuck and where you've made progress, even when it feels like the fog is thick.

Getting started with the 90-Second Journal is straightforward, which is key when anxiety is high and motivation low. You don't need an elaborate setup—just a small notebook or a notes app on your phone works perfectly. The real magic happens in the moment, right after you notice your anxiety climbing or a panic feeling swirling up. That's when you pause. You write. You press "pause" on the runaway thoughts.

Here's a simple way to structure each entry:

1. **What am I feeling right now?** Be honest and specific. Instead of "I'm anxious," try "My chest feels tight, and I'm worrying about tomorrow's meeting." Naming your sensation vividly makes it more manageable.

2. **What triggered this feeling?** This step helps draw connections between events or thoughts and how they impact your mood. Saying, "I saw an email about extra work," or "I remembered the argument earlier," starts to uncover what sparks your anxiety.

3. **How am I responding or how would I like to respond?** This might be noting a grounding tool you used, a breathing exercise, or a mental shift you want to practice next time. This turns the journal into a roadmap for change.

Because the journal is brief, it avoids overwhelming you with too much introspection. Instead, it encourages a steady habit—small, consistent check-ins that build your awareness muscle. You don't have to write perfectly or deeply analyze everything. The goal is simply to catch anxiety in action and start rewriting your mental responses.

Even if you don't feel like writing, just a few words or bullet points can do the trick. The act of putting thoughts outside your head interrupts the endless internal chatter and creates a bit of mental breathing room. Over time, this breaks the panic loop described in Chapter 1—you go from reactive to reflective, from trapped to empowered.

Another crucial benefit of the 90-Second Journal is how it nurtures self-compassion. Anxiety often comes with harsh self-judgment—"Why can't I just calm down?" or "Why am I so weak?" Logging your feelings regularly allows you to watch your brain's habit patterns without blaming yourself. You start to see that anxiety is a puzzle, not a personal failing. And that realization is a huge step toward healing.

Tracking your experiences might also reveal unexpected insights. Perhaps certain situations or times of day consistently push your anxiety higher. Maybe particular coping strategies work better for you than others—and having a written record makes those truths easier to remember and apply. This kind of personalized knowledge is empowering, giving you the tools to customize your anxiety management in a way that fits your life.

Some people worry that journaling will just amplify their worries, but the 90-Second Journal is designed to prevent that pitfall. The focus isn't on ruminating or digging into heavy emotions but on quick, clear-eyed notes that promote understanding and control. By keeping entries brief and purpose-driven, you avoid slippery slopes of overthinking.

You don't have to do this journal perfectly or every single time you feel anxious. The power lies in the habit, not the precision. Whenever you remember, wherever you are, just pull out your journal, spend 90 seconds, and capture a snapshot of your inner state. The more you practice, the stronger and steadier your emotional resilience becomes.

For those moments when panic feels overwhelming, this tool serves as a gentle anchor. Rather than fighting anxiety head-on, you're engaging it with curiosity and care. This approach aligns with the overall philosophy throughout this book: that anxiety isn't something to battle or erase but something to understand and gently guide toward calm.

By weaving The 90-Second Journal into your daily routine, you're building a bridge between reacting and responding. You're training your brain to notice anxiety's subtle signals before they spiral out of control. This simple, quick practice becomes a foundation for longer-term rewiring and mental freedom, which we'll explore more in the next chapter.

Remember, the journal doesn't have to be perfect or profound. Its strength is in its consistency and immediacy. Think of it as hitting the mental "reset" button in under two minutes. Over time, these small moments accumulate, gradually reshaping how your brain interprets stress and anxiety.

So, grab a notebook, set a reminder on your phone, or use a notes app. The 90-Second Journal is waiting to help guide you out of the panic loop and into a calmer, clearer state of mind—one brief entry at a time.

DR. AVA KINGSLEY, PSYD

TOOL 8: MICRO-MOVEMENT FOR MAXIMUM CALM

When anxiety strikes, sometimes the smallest actions can make the biggest difference. Micro-movement is a simple, yet incredibly powerful tool designed to help you regain control and calm your nervous system within seconds. It's about engaging your body in subtle, intentional motions that prompt your brain to shift out of panic mode and into a state of grounded calm. These movements aren't about breaking a sweat or doing full workouts—they're tiny, precise gestures you can do anywhere, anytime, even in moments of intense distress.

Why does micro-movement work so well for anxiety? When your body senses movement, it sends signals to your brain that life is safe, not threatening. Anxiety often traps you in a freeze or fight-flight cycle, but shifting your muscles—even slightly—breaks that cycle. These small physical cues interrupt the anxious feedback loop your brain keeps replaying. Think of it as a quick reboot. Instead of knocking you off balance, micro-movements restore equilibrium, anchoring your mind back to the present moment.

One of the unique strengths of this tool is its accessibility. When panic or anxiety spikes, it might feel impossible to take a long walk or do yoga poses. Micro-movement steps in because they are discrete, easy to perform without anyone noticing, and can be done seated, standing, or lying down.

You don't need any equipment, special clothing, or even space. Just a willing body and a moment's attention.

The key lies in focusing on controlled, deliberate movement. This isn't about random fidgeting or restless pacing. Instead, you'll work with targeted muscle groups and specific motions designed to activate a calming response. For example, gently rotating your wrists or softly tapping your fingers against your palm sends gentle proprioceptive signals to your brain. These signals help override your body's fight-or-flight signals, nudging your nervous system toward relaxation.

Let's get practical. You might begin by simply lifting one hand and making slow, circular movements at your wrist. Notice how even this tiny shift pulls your focus away from spiraling thoughts and into the sensation of moving flesh and bone. This redirection is crucial. Anxiety thrives on rumination and worry loops, and distractions that engage your body help break these chains.

Similarly, small shoulder rolls can relieve the tension that often builds in moments of stress. Just a few gentle rotations backward and forward send calming feedback to your brainstem, which regulates autonomic functions like heart rate and breathing. Catching those subtle contractions and releases reinforces a sense of physical grounding. Don't underestimate the power of relaxed muscles in signaling a safe environment to your anxious brain.

Another excellent micro-movement is seated foot taps. Tapping your feet lightly against the floor, one at a time, creates a rhythm that connects your body to the ground. It's a simple sensory input that provides a steady beat for your nervous system to sync with. Your brain appreciates this kind of consistency amid the chaos of anxious racing thoughts. Over time, repeating these taps for 90 seconds can be like hitting the mute button on mental noise.

Micro-movements also prime the parasympathetic nervous system—that branch responsible for "rest and digest." Activating this system helps slow your heartbeat and deepen your breathing naturally without forcing it. Think of it as a side door into calm, bypassing the usual stress triggers that heighten panic.

While micro-movement is subtle, it's incredibly adaptable. You can tailor these movements to your own body's needs and preferences. Some people might find gentle finger stretches more soothing, while others prefer slow head tilts combined with neck rotations. The goal is to find what feels good and helps you tune into your body—something many anxious minds overlook. When you make contact with the body this way, you step out of your headspace and into your physical presence.

At times, those struggling with anxiety may avoid movement altogether, fearing it will exacerbate their symptoms. Micro-movement offers a gentle invitation back into the body. It's a reminder that your body and mind are allies, not enemies. When anxiety feels overwhelming, these tiny gestures are simple ways to reconnect and reassure yourself that you're okay in this moment.

Consistency is another pillar of success with micro-movement. Integrating these small exercises into your daily routine—even when you're not feeling anxious—builds familiarity and strength. Your brain begins to associate these motions with calm and resilience. Then, when panic creeps in, your brain will quickly turn to these tools as natural coping mechanisms, reinforcing positive patterns over time.

You might wonder how to start incorporating micro-movement without it feeling like a chore. Begin small: select two or three movements you can do daily. Practice them each morning or during natural breaks in your day. The simplicity of this approach makes it sustainable and far more likely to stick, unlike complicated routines that quickly fall by the wayside.

In moments when you feel a panic attack rising, micro-movement offers a discreet solution. You can engage these techniques while waiting in line, sitting at your desk, or even during conversations. The subtlety means there's no pressure or embarrassment—just a quiet way to regain your center and breathe easier.

It's also worth noting that micro-movement pairs beautifully with other calming tools. For instance, when combined with tactical breathing or grounding techniques, your body and mind receive multiple layers of reassurance.

DR. AVA KINGSLEY, PSYD

This combined approach accelerates the calming process and strengthens your overall toolkit against anxiety.

Don't be surprised if, after practicing micro-movement, you notice an increase in body awareness beyond just anxiety relief. Many people report feeling more present, more connected to their physical sensations, and even more energized. These benefits extend well beyond the 90-second window, enhancing your overall mental wellbeing.

Recognize too that micro-movement is a tool of empowerment. Instead of waiting for anxiety to pass on its own, you take an active role in calming yourself. This subtle reclaiming of control is vital because anxiety often makes you feel powerless. When you engage your body in this way, you carve out a safe space where panic loses its hold.

In summary, micro-movement works by shifting your brain's focus, interrupting anxious patterns, and signaling safety through gentle, deliberate motion. It's accessible, versatile, and most importantly, effective. Taking just 90 seconds to move with intention invites calm to enter your nervous system—even when the storm feels overwhelming.

Give yourself permission to try these small but mighty gestures. See them not as tasks or obligations but as moments of kindness toward your body and mind. When anxiety threatens to take over, micro-movement is there to help you regain peace without needing hours of therapy or complex techniques. Sometimes, the smallest moves can spark the biggest change.

TOOL 9: THE 1-MINUTE MINDSET RESET

When anxiety strikes, sometimes all it takes is a tiny shift to stop the spiral before it deepens. That's exactly what the 1-Minute Mindset Reset is designed to do. This tool focuses on transforming your immediate frame of mind in just sixty seconds, offering a quick yet powerful way to regain control and calm when panic looms.

This reset is not about complex techniques or lengthy meditation sessions. Instead, it leans into the idea that your mindset, the lens through which you view a stressful situation, has an enormous impact on how anxiety expresses itself. When you learn to interrupt negative or catastrophic thoughts quickly, you weaken anxiety's grip and create space for clearer thinking.

Begin by recognizing that the way you talk to yourself matters deeply. That internal dialogue can either fuel panic or ease it. The 1-Minute Mindset Reset encourages deliberate self-talk designed to challenge and reframe anxiety-driven narratives.

First, take a moment to acknowledge what's happening emotionally and physically inside you. This awareness isn't about judgment or trying to "fix" things immediately. Instead, it acts like a spotlight, shining on your current experience with curiosity. For example, you might internally say, "I feel tense and worried, and that's okay for now."

By giving yourself permission to notice anxiety without panic, you interrupt the automatic response that often escalates it. This simple act of acknowledgment buys you valuable seconds to slow down and assess instead of reacting impulsively.

Once you've observed your state calmly, it's time to shift your focus. The 1-Minute Mindset Reset encourages you to mentally walk yourself through a brief sequence of empowering statements or questions that redirect your thoughts.

1. **Question the certainty:** Ask yourself, "Is this fear based on fact or assumption?" Anxiety thrives in "what-ifs" and worst-case scenarios. A quick reality check often reveals these thoughts are exaggerated.

2. **Recall past strength:** Remind yourself of moments you have managed anxiety successfully in the past. This taps into your resilience and builds confidence, even if the current situation feels tough.

3. **Focus on what you control:** Instead of wandering down roads of uncertainty, ground your attention on actionable steps or things within your reach right now.

This mental triage, all packed into about sixty seconds, pauses the emotional flood and rewires your brain's response over time. The technique aligns beautifully with how anxiety neurons fire fast – the moment you interrupt them, you open pathways to calm.

Don't underestimate how powerful this reset can be. Even though it's brief, the act of intentionally steering your mindset is a form of mental muscle-building. Just like physical exercise strengthens the body over time, these quick mindset shifts strengthen your brain's ability to manage anxiety more effectively.

Here's a practical way to practice the 1-Minute Mindset Reset. When anxiety flickers or catches you off guard:

- Stop whatever you're doing for a moment.
- Take a slow, deep breath, and silently acknowledge your feelings ("This is anxiety, and I'm safe right now").
- Gently push back against the anxiety thoughts by questioning them ("Is this really true? What evidence do I have?").
- Recall one instance where you handled something tough before.
- Focus on a single thing you can control in the immediate moment, no matter how small.

In less than a minute, you'll be rewiring your brain's reaction to stress. This isn't about convincing yourself that anxiety isn't real or significant. Instead, it's about shifting the energy away from fear-driven catastrophizing toward grounded reality and personal empowerment.

One of the key reasons this tool works so well is its simplicity and accessibility. It doesn't require preparation or special settings. Whether you're stuck in traffic, sitting at your desk, or waiting in line at the store, you can pull out this reset whenever needed.

Another important aspect is consistency. Using the 1-Minute Mindset Reset regularly strengthens the pathways for calmer thinking. Anxiety often hijacks us because our brains default to the same survival circuits. By rewiring those habits daily—even moment to moment—you reclaim control over your mental landscape.

Over time, this reset fosters a healthier relationship with your anxiety. Instead of viewing panic attacks or anxious moments as overwhelming crises, you start to see them as signals to pause, reset, and respond differently. That perspective alone reduces the intensity and frequency of symptoms.

It's also worth noting that this tool naturally complements other methods in your anxiety toolkit. For example, after grounding through your senses or tactical breathing, the mindset reset is a neat follow-up that aligns your thoughts with the calm state you've already begun to create.

We all face moments when anxiety tries to convince us that the worst is inevitable or that we are powerless. The 1-Minute Mindset Reset interrupts that narrative by reminding you that thoughts are just thoughts—they aren't facts or commands. You get to decide which ones you listen to.

STOP ANXIETY NOW

Imagine the freedom in knowing you hold this mental switch at your fingertips. Rather than feeling at the mercy of your brain's alarm system, you become an active participant in managing your inner experience.

If anxiety is a storm, this reset acts like a moment of stillness in the eye—quiet, centered, and empowering. It gives you the chance to choose your next step rather than being swept away.

Practice is key. The first few attempts might feel awkward or less effective. That's totally normal. Your mind is used to running the anxiety scripts. But every time you interrupt and redirect, you weaken those scripts and help your brain learn new ways to respond.

In addition to helping manage immediate anxiety, the 1-Minute Mindset Reset promotes greater emotional intelligence. By pausing to notice and label thoughts, you become more attuned to how your mind operates. This awareness lays the foundation for bigger shifts down the road.

Remember, this tool is designed for moments when you need instant relief—not to replace longer-term strategies like therapy, self-care routines, or medication if prescribed. It's a handy, accessible way to take back your calm right now, wherever you are.

If you're ready to take charge of your anxiety one minute at a time, the 1-Minute Mindset Reset is a powerful ally. Start practicing it today, and you'll be surprised how even

DR. AVA KINGSLEY, PSYD

the briefest moment of intentional pause can create a ripple effect of calm throughout your day.

TOOL 10: EMERGENCY EXIT PLAN (FOR HIGH-INTENSITY MOMENTS)

When anxiety spikes into full-blown panic, the situation can feel overwhelming and out of control. You might feel like you're spinning too fast, unable to catch a breath or think straight. That's exactly when having an Emergency Exit Plan becomes a crucial lifeline. This tool is designed for moments when your normal coping strategies just aren't enough—when anxiety hits so hard that you need a rapid, reliable way to step back, regroup, and regain control.

The Emergency Exit Plan isn't about avoiding your anxiety or running away from it forever. Instead, it offers a powerful way to hit the "pause" button—giving you immediate relief so you can stay safe mentally and emotionally, even in the most intense moments. Imagine knowing you have a clear, step-by-step method to pull yourself out of the anxiety storm, no matter how high the intensity. That peace of mind alone can change how you experience panic attacks.

This tool works because high-intensity anxiety activates your body's fight-flight-freeze response, flooding your system with stress hormones. Your brain short-circuits typical reasoning and logic, and your physical sensations become so loud that they drown out your thoughts. The Emergency Exit Plan works by interrupting this cascade, helping you regain conscious control in about 90 seconds—when your brain is still flexible enough to recalibrate and steady your nervous system.

Start by recognizing signs that a high-intensity moment is unfolding. Maybe your heart races, your chest tightens, or your thoughts race into worst-case scenarios. These early cues give you precious seconds to initiate your plan before panic takes full hold. Preparing yourself ahead of time with this plan means you won't have to think or analyze under pressure—you'll have a go-to strategy preloaded, ready for immediate action.

Here's one simple, effective way to build your Emergency Exit Plan:

1. **Anchor Yourself with a Safe Space:** Identify a location where you can take a few moments to yourself. It might be a quiet corner at home, a restroom stall, a park bench, or even your car. This is your mental and physical refuge, a place where distractions are minimized, and you can focus solely on regulating your state.

2. **Engage Your Five Senses:** Use a grounding technique rooted in sensory awareness to pull your mind entirely into the present. Name out loud or in your head five things you see, four things you hear, three things you feel, two things you smell, and one thing you taste. This sensory checklist reconnects your brain with reality and pulls you away from spiraling thoughts.

3. **Complete Tactical Breathing:** Slow down your breathing intentionally. Try inhaling deeply for four

seconds, holding your breath for four, exhaling slowly for six, then pausing for two seconds before repeating. This specific rhythm calms your nervous system, activating your parasympathetic state to counteract panic.

4. **Use a Comfort Object or Phrase:** If you have something comforting on hand—a small stone, a fidget tool, a necklace—hold it tightly. Alternatively, prepare a simple phrase that soothes you like, "This will pass," or "I am safe right now." Repeating this can ground your mind with reassurance.

5. **Give Yourself Permission to Step Away:** Sometimes, the bravest thing you can do is to remove yourself temporarily from stressful situations. Avoid self-judgment or guilt about stepping back. Anxiety doesn't mean weakness; it means you need to regroup to take your next steps more strongly.

This plan isn't just about what you physically do but also about strengthening your mindset toward anxiety. Having an Emergency Exit Plan reminds you that you don't need to endure all discomfort nonstop. You have agency, and sometimes taking a purposeful, controlled break is what helps you regain that power.

Let's break down why each piece of the plan is so critical during those moments:

- **Safe Space:** Anxiety hijacks your brain's reasoning center, triggering a survival mode that can feel utterly suffocating. Being somewhere you feel physically safe helps soothe your limbic system—the seat of emotions—and puts your body on the path to calming.

- **Five Senses Grounding:** Panic clouds your perception with fear-based scenarios that aren't rooted in the present. Sensory grounding forces your brain to reorient toward what's real here and now, dissolving the illusion created by anxious thoughts.

- **Tactical Breathing:** Because panic makes breath shallow and rapid, slowing and deepening your breathing acts like an off switch for the adrenaline flood. When your breath steadies, your heart rate follows, and the brain can function more rationally.

- **Comfort Tools and Phrases:** Familiarity provides safety. Sensory objects and calm mantras physically and mentally remind you that you're not alone and that this moment won't last forever.

- **Permission to Exit:** Many people feel pressure to "push through" panic, fearing they'll be judged or seen as weak. Recognizing it's okay to stop or remove yourself gives you permission to protect your mental health without shame.

It's important to practice this Emergency Exit Plan before you actually need it. Familiarity makes a huge difference; when you rehearse these steps regularly, your brain stores the sequence as a trusted tool rather than an unfamiliar exercise. Like any emergency drill, the more you use it, the easier and quicker it becomes to slip into the routine when panic strikes.

Beyond immediate rescue, having this strategy reinforces a critical shift in your anxiety relationship. It changes the feeling of helplessness by building confidence that you can handle intense emotions, and you can survive moments that once felt unbearable. That shift alone can reduce the frequency and severity of panic, as your brain learns you have effective ways to calm itself.

It helps to think of your Emergency Exit Plan as a mental first aid kit: compact, portable, and always available. No matter where you are or what's happening, you can carry these steps with you silently, ready to deploy. The plan also dovetails with other 90-second tools you've learned, amplifying your overall toolkit for anxiety relief.

Sometimes, moments call for a faster exit, and other times, you might need to take more time to slowly rebuild. Either way, the emergency exit is never about "giving up." It's about honoring your body, mind, and emotions while choosing self-care and compassion. By responding to your anxiety with kindness and decisive action, you decrease its power over you.

Finally, remember that an Emergency Exit Plan works best when combined with broader, ongoing strategies in this book. It's a vital safety net during crises, but long-term rewiring and mindset resetting will make these emergencies less frequent in the first place. Using this tool regularly creates a feedback loop: each successful exit rebuilds your nervous system's resilience and wears down panic's hold over time.

You don't have to get through high-intensity anxiety moments by grit alone. Let your Emergency Exit Plan be a trusted friend—one that helps you step away, breathe deeply, and come back stronger.

Chapter 3
Rewiring the Brain for Long-Term Change

Changing how your brain handles anxiety isn't about overnight miracles—it's about understanding that your brain is wired to learn and adapt, which means long-term change is absolutely possible. By consistently practicing small, intentional shifts, you can create new neural pathways that weaken old, anxious patterns and strengthen calmer, more resilient ones. This process, called neuroplasticity, makes lasting relief more accessible than you might think, especially when combined with daily habits that support your mental health, like managing sleep, nutrition, and screen time. Instead of battling anxiety head-on, the goal is to gently talk to it, reshape your responses, and build new habits that stick, so over time anxiety loses its grip and you regain ownership of your days.

DR. AVA KINGSLEY, PSYD

THE BRAIN IS A PATTERN MACHINE: HOW TO REWIRE IT

Your brain is, at its core, a pattern machine. It's constantly scanning the world around you for familiar signals, connections, and habits. This isn't some flaw or quirk—it's a survival feature built over millions of years. When your brain finds a pattern, it's able to make predictions and keep you safe from harm. But for those struggling with anxiety or panic attacks, the patterns that form can become traps, triggering worry and fear even when there's no real danger.

Think about how often your brain jumps to conclusions during anxious moments. It might notice a racing heartbeat and immediately connect it to "something is wrong." Or a small feeling of dizziness spirals into a flood of catastrophic thoughts. These reactions happen because your brain has learned to associate certain physical sensations or thoughts with anxiety. The difficult part is that the brain doesn't always know if these threats are real or imagined—it just follows its programmed patterns. That means it can get stuck in loops of panic that feel impossible to break.

But here's the good news: the brain's love for patterns also means it can learn new ones. This is where neuroplasticity comes in—the brain's ability to rewire itself throughout life. You can teach your brain to recognize different cues, respond in healthier ways, and eventually, change anxious habits into calm, grounded ones. It's not about wiping away anxiety completely, but about shifting the response, so panic has less control over your life.

When you're rewiring your brain, it helps to understand why patterns are so sticky. Repetition plays a huge role. Every time a certain thought or behavior gets repeated, the neural connections strengthening that pattern grow stronger. Think of it like paths in the woods: the more you walk a path, the clearer and easier it becomes to follow. The less-used paths fade away. Anxiety forms in the same way, by walking the same mental "paths" over and over.

But here's the exciting part—just as old patterns get stronger through repetition, new patterns do, too. When you practice a new tool or strategy consistently, those new neural pathways become your brain's preferred route. Over time, your brain prioritizes these healthier responses, making anxiety less automatic and more manageable.

It's important to be patient with yourself during this process. Your brain isn't magically rewiring overnight—it takes time and consistent effort. When you try a new way of responding, the first few attempts might feel awkward or forced. That's completely normal. Like learning any new skill, the brain needs practice before new patterns become natural.

One reason many people get stuck in anxiety is because the old patterns get reinforced by habit. If every time you feel anxious, you avoid the situation or try to suppress the feeling, the brain learns that anxiety is dangerous and must be escaped. But avoidance essentially tells your brain to keep that pattern—the "danger" hasn't been disproved. Instead, intentionally stepping into new experiences, even if they provoke anxiety, gives your brain a chance to update its expectations. This doesn't mean pushing yourself into overwhelming situations, but rather gently challenging the old patterns so the brain can practice a new response.

Another key element is awareness. Your brain can't change patterns if it doesn't recognize them. That's why mindfulness and tracking your feelings are so powerful. When you notice the first signs of anxiety and label them, you create space between your experience and your reaction. That tiny pause gives your brain a chance to choose a different pattern—a less automatic, more thoughtful response. Over time, these moments add up and create lasting change.

It helps to think of rewiring as forming new habits for your nervous system—not just your mind. Anxiety can live in both your thoughts and your body. Patterns show up as tense muscles, shallow breathing, or a racing heart. When you practice calming your body through breathing or gentle movement, you're helping your brain associate these physical signals with calm instead of panic. This kind of integrated retraining is powerful because it addresses the whole system, not just one part.

What's exciting about the brain as a pattern machine is the power this gives you. You're not stuck with the way things are now. Even if your anxiety feels overwhelming right now, you can gradually retrain your brain's responses.

STOP ANXIETY NOW

The 90-second tools you've learned earlier in this book are designed to interrupt those old anxiety loops and start forming new patterns right at the moment panic tries to take over. Each time you use them, you're practicing rewiring your brain in real time.

Rewiring the brain also means changing your expectations about anxiety itself. Instead of constantly fighting or fearing it, you can learn to "talk" to anxiety differently—even welcome the opportunity to change your mental patterns. This mindset shift makes rewiring less of a chore and more of an empowering journey. You're not broken or weak; your brain is just adapting to survive with a particular style. Now, it's time to teach it a better way.

Remember, patterns form naturally, but they don't have to stick forever. With attention, practice, and kindness toward yourself, your brain can learn new routes to navigate anxiety. Over time, those alternative paths become easier to take, and the old, fearful ones lose their grip. This is how long-term change happens—a steady building of new habits that outshine anxiety's hold.

So when anxiety tries to hijack your mind, remind yourself that your brain is listening and learning. Each moment you use a tool, pause instead of reacting, and choose a new way forward, you're strengthening your capacity to overcome panic. The brain may be a pattern machine, but it's also the most adaptable organ you have. That means

DR. AVA KINGSLEY, PSYD

every small step you take is rewiring your brain for calm, confidence, and control.

NEUROPLASTICITY IN ACTION: SMALL SHIFTS, BIG WINS

When it comes to rewiring your brain for long-term change, it's easy to think you need massive overhauls or deep, complicated interventions. But the truth is, neuroplasticity—the brain's natural ability to change—thrives on small, consistent shifts. These tiny, intentional changes add up over time, reshaping your neural pathways in ways that help reduce anxiety and calm panic attacks. Instead of waiting for some dramatic breakthrough, you can start making immediate, accessible tweaks that create big wins in your mental well-being.

Imagine your brain like a network of trails. At first, the well-worn paths are those anxious reactions and habitual panic responses. Each time you feel triggered and react, you're reinforcing those old trails. But neuroplasticity means you can build new trails—ones that lead to calm, control, and confidence. The catch? These new pathways don't appear because you want them to overnight. They form through repetition of small, healthier responses. With a bit of patience and the right focus, you're effectively editing the map your brain uses every day.

For people struggling with anxiety or panic attacks, these small shifts can feel incredibly empowering. You don't have to overhaul your entire life or dig deep into years of trauma to start seeing changes. Instead, practicing quick tools and making slight adjustments in your thinking, breathing, and reactions gently nudges your brain toward creating stronger, more positive connections. The exciting part is how these tweaks not only manage symptoms but also prevent future flare-ups by changing how your brain anticipates and processes stress.

One of the biggest misconceptions about rewiring the brain is that it requires hours of meditation, complicated therapy, or months of intense focus. While those things can be helpful, they're not the only path to change. Science shows that even 90-second interventions, repeated daily, can trigger neuroplastic changes. Because your brain is constantly adapting, even little moments count. Turning to quick grounding techniques, brief breath work, or micro-movements during a stressful moment interrupts anxious patterns and lays down fresh neural pathways. This is neuroplasticity at work.

Consistency is the key to these small shifts. It's not about doing everything perfectly or avoiding anxiety completely—that's not realistic. Instead, it's about giving your brain repeated opportunities to try a new response. Over time, your brain will favor those healthier connections and begin to let old anxious pathways fade into the background. This process doesn't erase anxiety overnight, but it changes how your brain handles it day by day, reducing its power over your life.

For example, a quick breathing technique performed during an anxious moment might seem too simple to have a lasting impact. But if you practice that tool consistently, every time anxiety creeps in, you're training your brain to recognize a different, calmer way to respond. Neuroplasticity rewards repeated practice by strengthening those new neural routes. What started as a small shift becomes a big win as you gain control over your anxiety rather than feeling controlled by it.

Another win comes from subtle changes in mindset. When you gently shift your thinking from catastrophic "what if" scenarios to grounded "what is" realities, you're rewiring how your brain interprets stress and threat. It's like teaching your brain a new language—one of safety and possibility instead of fear and shutdown. Because your thought patterns physically shape your brain's networks, these mindset tweaks create a foundation for lasting emotional resilience.

Incorporating micro-movements or body-based relaxation exercises might also sound minor, but they have a profound effect on your nervous system. Your brain's chemistry and electrical activity respond quickly to signals from your body. When you tense and release muscles or engage in short, intentional movements, you send messages that it's safe to calm down. Repeated regularly, these physical shifts rewrite the connection between your body and emotions, easing panic's grip.

It's important to recognize that neuroplasticity works best when these small shifts aren't just random attempts but become part of a daily habit. Creating just five minutes dedicated to implementing these tools makes a huge difference. Those minutes serve as training sessions for your brain, helping it build and reinforce new circuits of calm and control. This approach is sustainable, realistic, and accessible for anyone feeling overwhelmed by anxiety.

Beyond your individual efforts, these small advances build momentum. Each time you succeed in swapping an anxious reaction for a calm one, it reinforces your confidence. Confidence itself becomes a driver of change, encouraging you to keep trying and practicing. Over time, the wins compound. Anxiety's hold weakens, replaced by a sense of empowerment and ownership over your emotional experiences.

Change doesn't mean erasing your past reactions or pretending anxiety never happens again. Instead, it means gradually reshaping how you respond. When panic starts to rise, those new neural pathways can guide you toward quicker recovery. Neuroplasticity is showing you a different route—one where anxiety isn't the default but a passing signal you manage effectively. That's a game-changer for anyone tired of feeling stuck in fear or overwhelm.

Keep in mind that setbacks don't cancel progress. Your brain's plasticity allows for flexibility. Sometimes you'll slip back into old patterns, and that's okay. What matters is returning to those small shifts and tools and keeping the practice alive. Each return to calm is like reinforcing the new trail you're carving through the forest of anxious reactions.

Ultimately, the power of neuroplasticity lies in its accessibility. You don't need special equipment, a huge time commitment, or complex therapies to start changing your brain. With a few intentional, daily practices that take less than two minutes, you can harness your brain's ability to adapt. This makes long-term anxiety management less daunting and more achievable—turning small steps into powerful transformations.

So when you feel overwhelmed by anxiety, remember that meaningful change is a series of small wins, not giant leaps. Neuroplasticity gives you that chance. By committing to those tiny daily shifts—whether it's through breathing, grounding, reframing thoughts, or moving your body—you're quietly but surely rewiring your brain for resilience. And each small victory brings you closer to owning every day with confidence and calm.

DR. AVA KINGSLEY, PSYD

BUILD A DAILY 5-MINUTE PRACTICE THAT ACTUALLY STICKS

When it comes to rewiring your brain for long-term change, consistency beats intensity every time. You might think that overcoming anxiety requires huge time commitments or radical lifestyle changes, but that's not the case. In fact, just five minutes a day of focused practice can create meaningful shifts in how your brain processes stress and anxiety. The trick is building a daily habit that feels doable and fits smoothly into your life, so it actually sticks—no matter how busy or overwhelmed you feel.

One of the biggest challenges when building any new habit is staying committed beyond the first few enthusiastic days. Most people get excited, dive in headfirst, then crash or burn out because the routine doesn't feel sustainable. That's why the five-minute timeframe matters so much. It's short enough to remove resistance—you won't dread it or see it as a burden. Instead, it feels like a mini oasis in your day, a tiny pocket of calm you can rely on.

To get started, choose a regular time that best suits your natural rhythm. Some people find early mornings peaceful and quiet, while others prefer winding down before bed. The goal here isn't perfection or strict scheduling but creating a recognizable pattern your brain can latch onto. When your brain expects that mini break daily, it begins associating the practice with safety and control. Over time, this leads to rewiring your automatic anxiety responses.

Another key to making your five-minute practice stick is simplicity. Pick one or two tools that resonate with you, something you actually want to do—not what you think you should do. This could be tactical breathing, a quick grounding exercise, or a brief journaling session to track your anxiety shifts. If you try to cram too many strategies into that short window, it becomes overwhelming. You want your brain to relax, not race trying to remember a complicated routine.

It also helps to keep in mind why this practice matters. Anxiety often convinces us that we're powerless or stuck in panic loops forever. But each small, conscious action you take rewires those pathways, replacing fear responses with calm, control, and curiosity. Five minutes a day might seem small, but that's exactly what makes it powerful. It's consistent, manageable change that chips away at anxiety's grip one step at a time.

To make it even easier, consider pairing your five-minute practice with another daily habit you already have—like brushing your teeth or making your morning coffee. This "habit stacking" technique creates natural reminders to trigger your practice without relying solely on willpower. For example, after brewing your coffee in the morning, sit down for five minutes of tactical breathing or a calming body scan. Linking new habits to established ones ensures you don't forget and builds a stronger routine faster.

Accountability can be hugely motivating as well. Whether it's sharing your goal with a trusted friend, joining an online community focused on anxiety relief, or even setting up a gentle reminder on your phone, external prompts help you stay on track. Just remember to keep accountability supportive rather than punitive. If you miss a day, treat it as a chance to learn, not a failure. Compassion fuels momentum more effectively than pressure.

While five minutes might feel like a drop in the bucket compared to the hours of anxiety you endure, it's exactly these focused moments that activate neuroplasticity—the brain's ability to rewire itself. When you practice calming your nervous system regularly, those new connections get stronger and start overriding the old fear circuits. You're literally retraining your brain to respond differently to stress, making your moments of panic less frequent and less intense over time.

What's really encouraging is that this process fits naturally into your daily life. You don't need to carve out an hour or attend special classes. All it takes is intentionality and the willingness to prioritize your mental well-being for just a few minutes every day. This small investment builds a foundation of resilience that extends far beyond the five minutes, showing up as improved emotional regulation, sharper focus, and greater confidence.

Recognizing progress in your practice can be a powerful motivator too. Keep a simple log or journal where you note how you feel before and after your five-minute session. Over weeks, you'll likely see shifts that might have been too subtle to notice otherwise—maybe you catch yourself thinking more clearly, or you drift out of an anxious spiral faster. These tiny wins add up and reinforce why sticking with the habit matters.

The beauty of this approach lies in its accessibility—anyone can do it regardless of age, fitness level, or experience with anxiety tools. Because it's brief, you're less likely to mentally resist it or avoid starting. And because it's regular, you build a sense of mastery and control, which counters the emptiness anxiety often leaves behind. The daily practice becomes a safe space you claim for yourself, a literal pause button amid life's chaos.

It's normal to experience days when your practice feels harder or less effective. Anxiety isn't a linear process; progress comes with ups and downs. But the five-minute practice provides a consistent anchor through those fluctuations. It invites you to show up for yourself regardless of circumstances, solidifying your relationship with calmness and self-compassion. That's what rewiring really looks like—steady, gentle change focusing on progress, not perfection.

If you ever find your motivation waning, revisit your "why." What brought you here? What are you working toward—more peace, freedom from panic, the ability to enjoy each day without dread? Holding on to that vision can rekindle your commitment and remind you just how impactful a few minutes daily can be. It's far from trivial when it comes to transforming anxiety from a controlling force into a manageable part of your life.

In summary, building a daily five-minute practice that sticks is about making change achievable and realistic. It's about showing up even when you don't feel like it, layering tiny shifts over time, and creating a routine that honors your needs and limitations. By committing to this manageable chunk of intentional calm, you harness the brain's neuroplastic power and take steady steps toward lasting anxiety relief. This is your opportunity to rewrite old patterns and reclaim control, one deliberate breath and moment of presence at a time.

SLEEP, FOOD, AND SCREENS: HIDDEN ANXIETY TRIGGERS

When it comes to rewiring your brain and making lasting changes to reduce anxiety, the obvious targets usually involve mental techniques and coping strategies. But some of the most influential factors are hiding in plain sight—sleep habits, what you eat, and how much time you spend glued to screens. These elements might seem unrelated to your anxiety at first, but their impact on your brain's wiring and daily mood is profound. Sort of like invisible switches that can either turn your anxiety up or down without you even realizing it.

Let's start with sleep because it's the cornerstone of mental health. When your sleep quality fades or you don't get enough rest, your brain enters a kind of survival mode. Anxiety thrives in this environment. Sleep deprivation triggers the amygdala—the alarm center of your brain—to become hyper-reactive. Instead of managing stress like a pro, your brain goes on high alert, which keeps anxiety levels elevated. Even one night of poor sleep can increase feelings of nervousness, irritability, or panic the next day. What's tricky is that anxiety itself messes with sleep, creating a vicious feedback loop.

But contrary to popular belief, it's not just about the number of hours you log. The consistency and quality of sleep matter just as much. Tossing and turning all night does little to reset your neural pathways or calm your nervous system. Long-term, this disrupts neuroplasticity—the brain's ability to rewire and form healthier patterns, the very mechanism this book focuses on empowering you to activate. Prioritizing consistent sleep hygiene, like fixed bedtimes and winding down tech-free before bed, primes your brain for better rewiring. It's not a luxury; it's a necessity if you want to balance anxiety more effectively.

Next, food plays a more direct role in anxiety than many realize. The brain runs on nutrients, and poor dietary choices can stoke the fire of anxiety in ways you might not expect. For example, high sugar intake causes blood sugar spikes and crashes, which can mimic and trigger anxiety symptoms like jitteriness, sudden heart palpitations, and mood swings. Caffeine, though often embraced for its boost, can push your nervous system into overdrive, making anxiety spike or prolonging panic attacks. These are perfectly natural brain and body reactions, but they create confusion when you're trying to figure out why anxiety hits at seemingly random times.

On the flip side, foods rich in omega-3 fatty acids, magnesium, and B vitamins help regulate neurotransmitters linked with mood and resilience to stress. You don't need to overhaul your entire diet overnight, but incorporating small, brain-supportive changes feeds not only your body but the neural networks you want to rewire. Think of it as providing your brain with the right fuel so it can build better, calmer pathways and manage anxiety more sustainably.

Now, screens—the double-edged sword of modern life—are another hidden anxiety trigger. Screens bombard your brain with endless streams of notifications, updates, and information, activating your brain's threat detectors constantly. This sustained low-level stress makes it difficult to calm down and break from anxious thought loops. Blue light exposure, especially before bedtime, suppresses melatonin, the hormone that signals your brain it's time to rest. Your brain's natural rhythm gets hijacked, making it harder to recover and rewire for calmness.

Besides, the habit of scrolling endlessly through social media or news feeds often fuels anxiety through exposure to unsettling or overwhelming content. It's an often overlooked factor because it feels like downtime or distraction, but repeated exposure can tweak your brain's threat perception, keeping anxiety circuits continually engaged. Setting boundaries around screen time—not just before bed but throughout the day—can create mental space for the brain to reset. It supports the rewiring process by reducing chronic stress signals that get in the way of forming new, calmer connections.

Understanding these hidden triggers helps you realize that rewiring the brain isn't just about calming thoughts or breathing exercises. To break free from anxiety patterns long-term, you have to address the environment in which your brain operates every day. Sleep, food, and screen habits create either a fertile ground for anxiety or a stable platform for healing. By shifting these patterns, you're fundamentally changing the conditions that influence your brain's neuroplasticity.

Imagine your brain as a garden: neuroplasticity is the soil's ability to grow new plants, but the garden's health depends on the quality of water and sunlight it receives. Poor sleep, junk food, and too much screen time are like drought, pests, and weeds. You want to nourish and protect your mental garden by adjusting these inputs so the plants of calm and confidence can flourish. And while it might feel overwhelming at first, the beauty is that small, consistent changes here act like powerful switches that rapidly improve your brain's capacity to manage anxiety.

It's also worth noting that some days you'll do better than others. Maybe you stay up late one night or indulge in comfort food when anxiety spikes or spend extra hours on your phone during a tough time. That's okay. What matters is the overall trend, the intentional rebalancing over weeks and months that makes a difference. The brain's wiring doesn't happen overnight, but establishing a foundation of better sleep, nourishing food, and mindful screen use accelerates your progress and keeps anxiety triggers at bay.

So, as you practice the 90-second tools to smash panic and rewire your brain, remember to treat your body and environment as partners in this process. Don't underestimate the power of turning off devices early, choosing meals that stabilize your mood, or committing to restful sleep routines. Each improvement in these areas lowers the volume of anxiety's signal and makes it easier for your brain to embrace the calm, resilient patterns you're actively building.

Ultimately, rewiring your brain for long-term change is about creating a lifestyle that supports mental health as naturally as possible. Sleep, food, and screens are silent players on this team—you won't see them in every anxiety toolkit, but they're absolutely essential. Paying attention to these hidden anxiety triggers gives you yet another edge to reclaim control, smash panic, and own every day with more peace and confidence.

DR. AVA KINGSLEY, PSYD

HOW TO TALK TO ANXIETY INSTEAD OF FIGHTING IT

When anxiety hits, the natural reaction is to fight against it. We push, resist, and try desperately to shut it down, like an unwanted enemy knocking at the door. But here's the catch: anxiety isn't really the enemy. It's a message, a signal from your brain that something's off, something it's trying to warn you about. Changing your approach from battling anxiety to talking with it can transform how your brain responds and start rewiring it for long-term change.

Fighting anxiety often ramps up your stress response. When you resist feelings of panic or worry, you ironically amplify them. Your brain interprets this resistance as a threat, triggering more adrenaline, faster heartbeats, and tighter muscles. This cycle can feel relentless. Instead, imagine treating anxiety like a curious child tapping you on the shoulder, trying to get your attention. By leaning in with curiosity and calm, rather than confrontation, you break the feedback loop that nerves you out and reset your system.

Talking to anxiety involves recognizing it as a part of you, not something alien to expel. This simple shift invites compassion rather than judgment. What if, instead of telling your anxiety to "go away," you asked it what it's trying to tell you? Anxiety often carries a fear or concern deeply rooted in survival wiring but can sound like a distorted alarm in daily life. Giving it space to be heard reduces its volume. When you listen, even silently, your brain starts to relax because it knows you're not ignoring or attacking the signal anymore.

This way of relating to anxiety aligns perfectly with the idea of neuroplasticity—the brain's incredible ability to rewire itself based on new patterns of response. Every time you respond to anxiety with confusion or anger, you reinforce fear pathways. When you respond with curiosity and kindness, you forge new neural trails that weaken anxiety's hold. It takes practice, but over time your brain rewires itself to approach anxiety less as a threat and more as a messenger. This is where real long-term change begins.

You might wonder what talking to anxiety actually looks like when the feelings surge and your chest tightens. It's not about having a full-on conversation in your head or trying to reason your way out of physical sensations. Instead, it's a softer, gentler awareness paired with simple, supportive self-talk. For example, when panic creeps in, instead of "Get out of my head!" try silently saying, "I see you're here. I'm safe." This doesn't negate the feeling but acknowledges it without judgment or panic. You're validating your experience without feeding the fight-or-flight reaction.

One powerful technique is to personify your anxiety. Give it a name, a shape, or an image that represents the feeling. When anxiety strikes, picture it in your mind's eye—not as a giant monster, but maybe like a small, nervous creature or a flickering flame. You can then mentally "talk" to this image. Ask questions like, "What are you worried about right now?"

or "What would you like me to know?" This might sound unusual, but it places you in the role of observer, making anxiety less overwhelming and more manageable.

Language matters here, too. Words shape our internal reality. Instead of commanding your anxiety to disappear, use phrases that invite cooperation. "I'm here with you," or "We're going to get through this together," sends a signal of partnership, not opposition. This kind of framing helps your brain shift from defensive to calm modes, which is crucial for breaking the loop of constant fear.

It might feel uncomfortable or counterintuitive at first. After all, anxiety is often urgent and loud, demanding quick fixes. But fighting it is like wrestling a wave—you exhaust yourself trying to push back. Talking to anxiety is more like bobbing with the tide, gently moving with its rhythm until the wave passes. This approach doesn't mean you're surrendering or giving in. Instead, it shows strength through acceptance and smart self-regulation.

In practical terms, developing this dialogue requires patience and intention. Start small. The next time anxiety rises, pause and take a deep breath. Bring to mind that internal dialogue with whatever kind, curious phrase feels right in the moment. Over time, these small interactions begin to reprogram your responses. Your brain learns that anxiety isn't a signal to panic but a feeling to be acknowledged and managed. This creates a sense of safety inside your nervous system, which is essential for rewiring anxiety pathways.

STOP ANXIETY NOW

Another key aspect is noticing your emotional tone when you "talk" to anxiety. Is your voice harsh or soft? Skeptical or accepting? Expressing irritation—even mentally—can backfire. Instead, soft, steady tones help soothe the brainstem where anxiety often takes root. Think of this as a form of self-compassion practice, where kindness toward your anxious parts invites healing. It sounds simple, but it's a powerful tool in retraining your brain's emotional habits.

Alongside this internal communication, physical strategies you've already learned—from tactical breathing to grounding—work best when paired with this mindset shift. Talking to anxiety is like opening a door; those 90-second tools can then flow through more easily, calming your nervous system faster. This dynamic duo primes your brain to relearn calmness at a fundamental level.

For many, the habit of fighting anxiety is deeply ingrained. It might feel strange or even frustrating to stop pushing so hard. But remind yourself that the goal isn't to eliminate anxiety overnight; it's to change your relationship with it. This makes all the difference. You're not stuck with a relentless enemy inside you. You're cultivating an uneasy but honest dialogue with a nervous part of yourself. That honesty, paired with patience, gently shifts your brain's wiring and opens the door to lasting change and improved well-being.

Lastly, remember that this process takes time. You won't always get it right, and some moments the fight impulse will surge back. That's okay. Recognizing when you're slipping into resistance is part of building awareness. Each time you catch yourself and return to a calm, curious dialogue with your anxiety, you're strengthening those new pathways. Gradually, anxiety loses its grip and becomes a less frightening—and less dominant—part of your mental experience.

Learning to talk to anxiety instead of fighting it is a transformative skill in your toolkit for conquering anxiety long-term. It rewires your brain to coexist with fear, rather than battle it endlessly. As you practice, anxiety stops feeling like an enemy and starts to feel more like a signal you can understand and manage. This subtle but profound shift moves you from a place of resistance to resilience, creating lasting change and opening the door to owning every day.

Chapter 4
Owning Every Day with Confidence

Taking control of your day when anxiety looms can feel like climbing a mountain, but confidence isn't about being fearless—it's about moving forward despite fear. By embracing small, intentional habits and using quick tools designed to ground you in the present, you build a foundation that supports resilience even on tough days. Confidence grows not from never feeling anxious but from recognizing your ability to face challenges head-on, adjusting your mindset, and borrowing strength when you need it most. This chapter shows how to lean into your own power every morning and throughout the day so anxiety loses its grip, letting you live with more ease and purpose—owning each moment as it comes.

DR. AVA KINGSLEY, PSYD

MORNING ROUTINES FOR AN ANXIETY-PROOF DAY

Starting your day right can make all the difference when it comes to managing anxiety. It's not about waking up perfect or having a flawless morning; rather, it's about setting a foundation that supports your mental well-being from the moment you open your eyes. A carefully crafted morning routine acts like a shield that helps cushion the impact of stress and panic as the day unfolds. When anxiety feels relentless, having predictable, calming rituals can bring a surprising sense of control and confidence—even in small doses.

You don't need to launch into an elaborate set of tasks. Think of your morning routine as a gentle protocol designed to ground and center you. This isn't about rushing or trying to cram productivity into the first few hours; it's about creating intentional moments that soothe your nervous system and prepare your brain to handle stress better. Even simple actions, repeated daily, have the power to rewire your brain's reaction to anxiety triggers, reducing the chance of panic spirals later.

Waking up in itself can be a challenge when anxiety is present. For many, the first thoughts that ripple through the mind might lean toward worry, dread, or a flood of "what-ifs." That's why the very first moments upon awakening are so critical. Without the right starting point, these automatic anxious thoughts can snowball quickly. A well-planned morning routine intervenes here, giving you tools to pause and slow down before the chaos begins.

One of the most effective ways to start your day is by focusing on your breathing. Tactical breathing exercises can be just the reset you need before even stepping out of bed. This technique, involving slow inhales and controlled exhales, sends a direct message to your brain that it's safe to relax. Integrating this into your morning calms the sympathetic nervous system—the part responsible for your fight-or-flight response. The trick is to keep it short and simple; even sixty seconds makes a difference.

Alongside breathing, grounding exercises invoke your senses to anchor you fully in the present moment. In practice, this might be as straightforward as noticing five things you can see in your bedroom, four sounds you can hear, or three things you can touch. These sensory checks interrupt anxious thought patterns from the start. Incorporating a mini grounding session into your morning routine gently shifts the brain away from worry and into awareness of the here and now. Over time, this becomes a powerful habit that weakens anxiety's grip.

Physical movement in the morning works wonders, too. You don't have to dive into intense workouts or lengthy yoga sessions. Even just a few minutes of stretching or mindful micro-movements can stimulate the vagus nerve, which plays a crucial role in calming your nervous system.

Simple actions—like raising your arms overhead, rolling your shoulders, or gentle neck stretches—help break the tension anxiety leaves in your body during sleep. Moving your body sends signals that you're ready to engage with your day, not get caught up in fear.

Hydration is another underestimated but valuable element of an anxiety-proof morning. Drinking a glass of water after waking replenishes what's usually lost overnight and supports your brain function. Low hydration can exacerbate symptoms like fatigue and irritability, which often fuel anxiety. While it's not a cure-all, staying hydrated primes your body for clearer thinking and emotional balance right out of the gate.

Besides physical activities and hydration, tuning into your mindset sets the tone for how you approach challenges. This doesn't mean forcing yourself into relentless positivity. Instead, lean into an attitude of gentle acceptance and curiosity about your feelings. You might start by silently acknowledging how you feel without judgment—"I'm feeling anxious, and that's okay"—rather than immediately fighting or avoiding those emotions. This approach reduces resistance and lessens anxiety's intensity over time.

One technique you could include in your morning ritual is a brief journaling practice. You don't need to write pages; a few lines will do. Jotting down your thoughts or setting a positive yet realistic intention for the day helps organize your mind. Writing reduces mental clutter and brings clarity to your priorities, which is essential when anxious thoughts tend to feel overwhelming and scattered. By naming specific goals or affirmations, you create a kind of mental roadmap to steer by, making the day feel less intimidating.

It's also helpful to keep some flexibility in your routine. Anxiety is unpredictable, and some mornings will feel tougher than others. If a full set of rituals seems too much one day, scale back to the essentials like breathing or a quick stretch. The goal is consistency, not perfection. Over time, this consistency builds a muscle of resilience that makes anxiety less dominant in your daily experience.

Technology can be a double-edged sword in the mornings. Many people instinctively reach for their phone, plunging into emails, social media, or news that can amp up anxiety. Instead, try to delay screen time as much as possible—even a brief pause before consuming information can calm your nervous system. Consider reserving the first 10 to 15 minutes of your day for yourself—no devices, no distractions. This quiet time reduces external pressures and centers you internally before connecting with the world's noise.

Creating a physical environment that supports your anxiety-proof morning also matters. Keep your space tidy, inviting, and comfortable to avoid sensory overload or chaos that subtly fuels panic. Simple adjustments like opening a window for fresh air, letting natural light in, and surrounding yourself with calming colors or objects can influence mood more than expected. These small environmental tweaks send subtle messages of safety and calm to your brain.

Another important part of your morning routine is nutrition. Choosing a balanced breakfast with protein, healthy fats, and complex carbs provides sustained energy without blood sugar spikes that trigger mood swings or anxiety symptoms. While eating habits aren't the sole factor in anxiety management, what you put in your body influences your brain chemistry and stress levels. Starting your day with intentional nourishment supports both physical and mental stamina for the hours ahead.

Don't underestimate the power of a short moment of mindfulness or meditation, even if it's just two or three minutes. Sitting quietly and focusing on your breath or repeating a calming phrase ignites relaxation pathways in the brain. This practice gradually rewires neural circuits to favor calm over panic. It's a simple, science-backed tool that fits seamlessly into any morning routine, regardless of how busy life gets.

Lastly, part of owning your day confidently includes setting boundaries before the day fully demands your attention. This could mean deciding which emails or tasks you'll address and which ones you'll postpone. Having a plan reduces the feeling of being overwhelmed by responsibilities and allows you to approach tasks with greater focus. Anxiety often thrives in uncertainty, so pre-planning creates a sense of order that soothes the anxious mind.

STOP ANXIETY NOW

    The goal of a morning routine is not to eliminate anxiety altogether—this isn't always realistic. Instead, it equips you with a daily armor of calm and clarity so that when anxiety comes knocking, it's less likely to crash your whole day. By embedding small but impactful habits into your first waking moments, you send a powerful message to your brain that you're in control. It's this sense of empowerment, built over time, that helps transform anxious mornings into ones filled with confidence and possibility.

DR. AVA KINGSLEY, PSYD

HANDLING SOCIAL ANXIETY IN REAL TIME

Social anxiety can strike suddenly. Whether you're walking into a meeting, joining a group conversation, or just entering a crowded room, that familiar wave of discomfort can feel overwhelming. The good news? You don't have to wait to "fix" things later or avoid these situations to feel better. Real-time tools can help you manage social anxiety right when it happens, giving you the confidence to own the moment instead of letting it own you.

One of the first game changers is recognizing that social anxiety is often fueled by your brain's natural fight-or-flight system. When you feel watched or judged, your body reacts as if you're in danger—even if the threat is only imaginary. This response isn't a reflection of who you are; it's a wired system getting triggered. Once you identify that, you can create space between the feeling and your reaction, allowing you to interrupt the spiraling anxiety right as it starts.

Grounding techniques are some of the simplest and most effective tools in these moments. For example, the 5-4-3-2-1 reset asks you to engage your senses and bring your focus back to the here and now. Name five things you can see, four you can touch, three you can hear, two you can smell, and one you can taste. It's surprising how quickly this practice cuts through the noise of anxious thoughts and roots you in reality, calming both mind and body.

STOP ANXIETY NOW

Breathing is another hidden powerhouse when social anxiety flares up. Your breath tends to get shallow and rapid during anxious moments, fueling the panic. Tactical breathing—slowing your inhales and exhales, aiming for about six breaths per minute—helps calm your nervous system. It's like hitting the reset button for your brain's alarm system. Even just a minute of focused breathing can reduce the racing heart and sweaty palms that often come with social situations.

When you notice negative or catastrophic thoughts about what others think of you, try an instant mental reframe. Instead of assuming the worst—like "Everyone thinks I'm awkward" or "I'm going to mess this up"—flip the script internally. Remind yourself that people are generally wrapped up in their own worlds and that one awkward moment won't define the whole interaction. This shift helps break the cycle before it escalates and gives space for more realistic, compassionate thoughts.

Social anxiety often whispers that you should avoid eye contact, stay quiet, or shrink away. But small, intentional micro-movements can flip that experience on its head. A slow, deliberate nod or a gentle smile can actually send signals to your brain that you're in control and safe. The body and mind communicate constantly; changing your posture or facial expressions can soften anxiety and boost your presence. These actions might feel a bit awkward at first, but over time they become natural confidence boosters.

DR. AVA KINGSLEY, PSYD

One tricky thing with social anxiety is how fast it can escalate. When you feel that swell of panic starting to intensify, having a quick exit plan can save you from spiraling further. This isn't about running away permanently; it's about giving yourself a brief timeout to recalibrate. That might mean stepping outside for a breath of fresh air, finding a quiet corner for a one-minute grounding exercise, or even sending yourself a calming text reminder. Knowing you have an emergency plan in place boosts courage to face social situations head-on.

Another real-time strategy is harnessing the power of curiosity instead of judgment. When you catch yourself stuck in "What if they're thinking this?" or "I'm going to say something dumb," try turning your attention outward. Ask yourself genuinely curious questions: "What is that person really talking about?" or "What's interesting about this group?" This subtle redirection prevents your mind from looping in fear and builds a natural ease in social settings.

There's a unique kind of strength that comes from accepting anxiety's presence without fighting it. When social anxiety arises, instead of battling every uncomfortable feeling, try a soft approach: acknowledge the discomfort and mentally say, "I notice you're here." It sounds simple but validating your experience lessens its power. Fighting anxiety tends to increase tension; accepting it—even as you act despite it—puts you back in the driver's seat.

In moments of social fear, self-compassion is a crucial ally. It's easy to judge yourself harshly when you stumble over words or feel awkward. Instead, remind yourself that everyone makes mistakes and that imperfection is part of human connection. An internal voice rooted in kindness helps reduce the shame or embarrassment that fuels future anxiety. Over time, practicing this kindness rewires your brain to respond more gently to social challenges.

Using these techniques in real time might feel challenging when you first try them. Social anxiety often creates a sense of urgency to escape or hide. But even practicing one or two tools consistently can build your confidence quickly. Each small victory—like making eye contact for a few seconds or staying in a conversation longer than you thought possible—strengthens your anxiety muscle. The more you face social situations equipped with helpful tools, the easier it gets.

Moreover, your brain learns through repeated experiences. Applying these strategies every time social anxiety shows up rewires your neural pathways to respond less fearfully. You're not trying to erase anxiety instantly; instead, you're training your brain to react with calmness and control. It's a powerful shift that turns social anxiety from a wall into a stepping stone.

Remember, social anxiety exists on a spectrum. Sometimes it flares mildly, other times it can feel intense. Tailor your real-time approach based on how you're feeling.

On tougher days, using grounding and breathing might be enough. In more challenging moments, adding an emergency exit or self-compassion statement can make a big difference. The key is having a mental toolkit ready, so anxiety doesn't catch you unprepared.

Social settings don't have to be battlegrounds. With the right strategies, they can become opportunities to practice owning your presence. Instead of shrinking away, you begin to show up and engage more authentically, little by little. Each interaction is a chance to build resilience and prove to yourself that anxiety doesn't have to control the outcome.

When you start embracing these real-time tools, you also reclaim your power over panic. Confidence isn't about never feeling anxious; it's about facing anxiety with intention and tools that work in the moment. This approach makes it possible to thrive socially, even when anxiety wants to push you backward.

Social anxiety isn't a sign of weakness—it's a challenge that millions face. But it doesn't have to stop you from owning your day. When you handle anxiety in real time, using straightforward and proven techniques, you unlock a new level of freedom. You begin to move through social situations with a sense of calm and purpose that feels genuinely your own. That's when owning every day shifts from being a wish to becoming your reality.

ANXIETY AT WORK: TOOLS FOR FOCUS AND CONFIDENCE

Work can be one of the biggest sources of anxiety for many people. Deadlines, meetings, constant emails, and the pressure to perform can feel overwhelming. When anxiety strikes in the middle of your workday, it doesn't just sap your energy— it can hijack your focus, leaving you spinning in a cycle of worry and overthinking. The good news is, you don't have to let anxiety call the shots at work. There are practical tools you can use right in the moment to regain control, sharpen your attention, and own your confidence, no matter the chaos around you.

First things first: recognize that feeling anxious at work is incredibly common. Anxiety shows up differently for everyone— some people feel jittery, others get stuck in a mental loop of "what ifs," and some experience physical symptoms like tightness in the chest or stomach knots. Understanding your unique anxiety patterns gives you the power to interrupt them quickly. One key approach is using brief, evidence-based techniques that fit seamlessly into your work routine. These tools aren't about pushing anxiety aside or pretending it's not there; they're about acknowledging the feeling, then redirecting your mind and body toward calm focus.

One of the simplest yet most effective tools you can use is tactical breathing. This technique, often called "box breathing," involves slowing down your breath to calm your nervous system in about 60 seconds. When you feel anxiety bubbling up during a tense meeting or before a presentation, quietly breathe in for four seconds, hold for four seconds, breathe out for four, and pause for four before starting again. This steady rhythm signals your brain to shift from fight-or-flight mode to a state of calm alertness. You can do this at your desk, in the bathroom, or even during a walk. The goal is to reclaim control of your body's physical response, which in turn brings your scattered thoughts into clearer focus.

Grounding techniques also shine as quick fixes for workplace anxiety. One reliable method involves tuning into your senses, right where you are. Take a moment to notice five things you see around you, four things you can touch, three things you hear, two things you smell, and one thing you taste. This sensory check-in pulls you out of the anxious spiral and anchors you firmly in the present. It's perfect for breaking the cycle of worry about future tasks, mistakes, or conversations. The more you practice, the faster your brain learns to flip the switch from overwhelm to calm attention.

Another game-changing tool is the instant reframe. Anxiety loves to twist thoughts into exaggerated dangers or worst-case scenarios. When you catch yourself caught in a spiral, gently stop and ask, "What's the evidence for this thought?" or "What's a more balanced way to look at this?" For example, instead of thinking, "I'm going to mess up this project and lose credibility," reframe to, "I'm prepared, and even if I make a mistake, I can fix it." These quick mental shifts break the negative feedback loop that feeds anxiety. Over time, they help rewire how your brain reacts to triggers.

Physical tension often rides shotgun with workplace anxiety. Maybe your shoulders pinch, your jaw clenches, or your hands tremble. Taking a brief moment to tense and release muscle groups can offer instant relief. Squeeze your fists tight for five seconds, then let go. Roll your shoulders back and down. These small movements interrupt the body's stress response and promote relaxation. Plus, they're subtle enough to do without drawing attention during a Zoom call or in the middle of a brainstorming session.

Sometimes, the best way to boost confidence at work is to change how you relate to your anxiety. Instead of viewing it as a roadblock or something to avoid, treat it as a signal— a messenger that tells you when you need to pause, recalibrate, or lean in differently. You might even start seeing anxiety as a kind of "early warning system" that prepares you to perform at your best. When you stop fighting the feeling and start listening, you unlock a fresh kind of courage: confident, grounded, and flexible.

Creating space for short breaks throughout your workday can also support focus and calm. It's tempting to power through from one meeting to the next, but pushing yourself nonstop fuels stress. Instead, schedule mini "check-ins" where you pause, breathe, and reset. These don't have to be long— just 60 to 90 seconds of intentional calm can reset your brain. Over time, these micro-pauses build resilience and keep anxiety from spiraling.

Remember, managing anxiety at work is not about perfection. It's about progress. Sometimes, you'll feel on top of your game; other times, anxiety will sneak in despite your best efforts. When that happens, use what I call the "borrowed strength" hack— reach out to a supportive colleague, mentor, or even a quick motivational phrase you've prepared. Hearing a kind word or reminding yourself of past wins can reignite your confidence when anxiety tries to dim your light.

It's also helpful to create an anxiety-friendly environment that supports your focus. Keep your workspace organized and free from clutter, use noise-cancelling headphones if distractions overwhelm you, and reserve certain times to check emails instead of constantly monitoring your inbox. These small environmental tricks can reduce sensory overload and allow your mind to settle.

One of the most important skills when managing anxiety at work is learning to prioritize tasks realistically. Overcommitting and trying to do everything perfectly feed anxiety's fire. Instead of piling on more work during stressful times, identify your most important tasks and focus on one at a time. Celebrate small wins as they come. This approach breaks down larger, intimidating projects into manageable, confidence-building steps.

Lastly, remember that building focus and confidence takes practice. Just as muscles grow stronger with exercise, your brain learns to handle anxiety better when you regularly apply these tools. Start by picking one or two techniques that resonate with you and experiment with them during your workdays. Notice how your energy shifts, how your mind clears, and how you build trust in your own ability to navigate stressful moments.

By weaving these practical anxiety-management tools into your daily work routine, you're not just surviving the day—you're owning it. You're shifting from being controlled by anxiety to guiding your own experience, reclaiming your focus, and stepping forward with real confidence. It's not about never feeling anxious again; it's about learning to rise above anxiety's grip and show up fully, exactly as you are.

DR. AVA KINGSLEY, PSYD

WHEN YOU'RE NOT FEELING STRONG— USE THE "BORROWED STRENGTH" HACK

There are days when anxiety hits hard, and your internal resources feel drained. You might wake up feeling fragile or find yourself in the middle of the day wondering how you'll push through the next hour, let alone the whole day. It's normal to feel this way, and it's not a sign of failure or weakness. Sometimes, your own strength just isn't enough in the moment—and that's precisely when the "borrowed strength" hack becomes a game-changer.

This technique is all about leaning in safely on external sources or internalized memories of strength, allowing you to draw from something outside yourself when your own reserves run low. It's a subtle shift that doesn't demand you to magically pull yourself up by the bootstraps. Instead, it invites you to connect with support or past experiences that can recharge your confidence, calm your nervous system, and remind your brain that you're capable—even when you don't quite feel it.

Imagine you're facing a wave of panic or a slump in motivation, and your usual coping tools just aren't cutting it right now. Borrowed strength means tapping into the energy, wisdom, or calm of someone you trust or a past moment when you overcame something tough. By doing so, you're not faking confidence—you're simply extending yourself the kindness of being supported, as if a trusted friend was right there with you.

One of the simplest ways to use borrowed strength is through visualization. It might feel too "woo-woo" if you're not used to it, but science supports how vividly recalling positive experiences or envisioning a powerful role model calms the amygdala—the brain's fear center—and activates areas that boost resilience. Picture someone who inspires you: it could be a family member, a friend, a mentor, or even a character from a book or movie whose courage or calmness you admire. Hold their presence in your mind and imagine how they would handle what you're going through right now.

This mental exercise flips your brain's panic response into a reassurance zone by sending signals that you're not alone, and there's someone wise to lean on. Remember, it doesn't have to be perfect or detailed. Even a vague sense of connection to that person's strength can calm the storm inside you.

Another form of borrowed strength is more practical—actually reaching out to your support system. Anxiety often whispers lies such as "You're alone" or "Nobody understands." Picking up the phone, sending a quick text, or even just being in the presence of someone who understands can make a huge difference. Sometimes just knowing that someone else is there can slow your racing thoughts and lower your heart rate. It's okay to let people in. Borrowing strength this way doesn't mean you're weak; it means you're smart enough to use resources available to you.

When external support isn't immediately accessible, internal borrowed strength can come from memories of past victories. You've faced challenges before, even if they're different from what you're experiencing now. Glimpse back at moments when anxiety didn't win. Maybe it was a presentation you nailed despite nerves, a difficult conversation you navigated calmly, or simply times when a panic attack passed and you survived—and thrived. Keep these memories at your mental fingertips to fuel your current fight. Remind yourself that you have already earned the right to keep going.

In those moments when even recalling past wins feels overwhelming, try anchoring borrowed strength in something tangible. Maybe it's a meaningful object—a piece of jewelry, a photo, or a small token—that reminds you of safety and support. Holding or seeing this item can ground you in a sense of belonging and perseverance, triggering your brain to shift from fight-or-flight mode toward calmer states.

Borrowed strength also works well with journaling prompts when spoken connection isn't possible. Write down the names of people you admire or recall encouraging words they've said in the past. List the qualities you wish to cultivate right now—courage, patience, calm—and imagine they're passing through you like a gentle but powerful current. This exercise deepens the psychological impact of borrowed strength by making it an active, tangible practice.

STOP ANXIETY NOW

It's important to acknowledge that borrowing strength doesn't erase your feelings or pretend anxiety isn't hard. Rather, it builds a bridge over that hard part so you can cross it when your own footing feels shaky. This approach doesn't mandate instant transformation or perfection. Instead, it offers a lifeline—a way to nurture yourself through tough patches without forcing solo heroism.

This technique closely aligns with the fundamental truth that no one owns confidence outright; it's not a finite resource stored inside of you alone. Confidence can expand through connections—to others, to memories, and even to imagined guides or mentors. Borrowed strength reminds you that you're not a lone island, and leaning on that truth can offer a quiet but powerful respite from anxiety's demands.

Interestingly, borrowed strength isn't only for moments of crisis. It can be a proactive tool for anxiety management throughout your day. When you begin your morning or step into a challenging social or work situation, briefly call to mind someone who embodies qualities you want to channel. This primes your brain to operate with calm and confidence, almost like mentally suiting up in armor before heading out into battle.

Finally, keep in mind that the borrowed strength hack is something you can customize endlessly. You might find pairing it with grounding tools or slow tactical breathing magnifies the effect. Or perhaps a quick mental pep talk from a mentor figure coupled with a one-minute journal entry shifts your mindset completely. Experiment with what feels right for you in the moment. The goal is to create personalized access points to strength that aren't dependent solely on your current emotional state.

By incorporating the borrowed strength strategy in your toolkit, you're creating a backup plan—a source of energy that you can tap into when your own feels depleted. This is not about hiding or masking your anxiety but about navigating it with kindness, resourcefulness, and the awareness that strength can come from many places beyond the self.

Next time you catch yourself feeling too overwhelmed to carry on, remember that you don't have to power through alone. Borrowed strength offers a scientifically supported, heartfelt method to steady your nerves and reclaim your confidence, even when those inner resources seem just out of reach. Owning every day with confidence doesn't mean never feeling vulnerable—it means knowing how to lean on the right support when you need it most, and borrowing strength is one of the quickest, most accessible ways to do exactly that.

LIVING BIGGER THAN ANXIETY: REDEFINING "BRAVE"

When anxiety is constantly knocking at your door, the word "brave" can start to feel like an impossible standard. Society paints bravery as grand gestures and fearless heroics, but anyone who lives with anxiety knows the truth is far more nuanced. Bravery isn't the absence of fear; it's taking action despite it. It's the quiet decision to face a day weighed down by worries, the deliberate choice to move forward when your heart races and your thoughts spiral. That kind of courage deserves recognition because it's so rarely seen or celebrated.

This section isn't about redefining bravery as some lofty, unattainable ideal. Instead, it's about recognizing the bravery you already live every single day. Bravery isn't just for the mountaintop moments or life-changing decisions—it's woven into the small, often invisible choices that keep anxiety from running your life. You're brave when you get out of bed, when you say "yes" to plans, or simply when you breathe through a panic attack instead of shutting down. Those aren't small victories; they're massive wins.

One major step in living bigger than anxiety is changing how you see yourself. Anxiety often comes with a harsh inner critic that calls you weak, broken, or incapable. But those labels couldn't be further from the truth. It takes strength to navigate life with anxiety. The effort it demands sometimes feels exhausting because it is. When you start to view bravery as persistence and resilience rather than perfection and heroics, it shifts your mindset and fuels a gentler, more compassionate way forward. This shift isn't automatic or easy—it takes practice. But that's the point. Bravery and growth happen in practice, in the day-to-day choices, not overnight.

Another important part of embracing this bigger idea of bravery is giving yourself permission to experience vulnerability. Showing up with honesty about your anxiety—whether to yourself or others—is a form of courage that can transform your relationship with your own struggles. Vulnerability releases the pressure to be "fine" all the time. It allows connection and support to grow instead of isolation and shame. When you share your truth, you're not only brave but creating a ripple effect that encourages others to do the same, building a more understanding community around mental health.

Living bigger than anxiety also means recognizing the moments when you need rest or support as acts of bravery—not weakness. Many with anxiety have been conditioned to think they must push through regardless of how bad it feels inside. That kind of mindset often leads to burnout and setback. Reframing rest as a strategic, powerful choice can make a huge difference. Asking for help, setting boundaries, and prioritizing self-care aren't signs that you're giving up; they're signs you're strong enough to protect your wellbeing so you can keep moving forward.

It's worth reflecting on how bravery with anxiety often looks very different from traditional ideas of what a "strong" person is. People without anxiety might find comfort in boldness and quick decisions, but for those of us managing anxiety, bravery may mean showing up slowly, step by step. Sometimes, it's simply holding space for discomfort without trying to escape it immediately. That persistence amid uncertainty can be exhausting, but it's a powerful form of courage. When you celebrate those moments as achievements, you're actively reshaping what bravery means in your life.

What would happen if you started framing your daily wins as proof of your courage? Every time you use one of the 90-second tools to interrupt a panic attack, every time you choose to face a feared situation instead of avoiding it, you're rewriting the narrative about what it means to be brave—with anxiety, and despite it. This new story isn't about flawless strength; it's about showing up imperfectly and refusing to let anxiety define you. It's about reclaiming control over how fear shapes your actions.

Sometimes, bravery means getting comfortable with uncertainty. Anxiety loves to keep you trapped in "what if" scenarios, convincing you that you must have all the answers before taking a step forward. But embracing bravery includes accepting that you don't have to be fearless or certain to keep going. You have permission to feel fear and move forward anyway. That kind of acceptance reduces the grip anxiety has on you, loosening its chains so you can do more of what matters.

Redefining bravery also means giving yourself credit for the strategies you've already developed to handle your anxiety, even if the progress has been slow or uneven. Maybe you've learned ways to ground yourself, to breathe through tension, or to interrupt negative thoughts. Each tool you use builds your skillset and resilience. When you recognize these efforts as brave choices, you empower yourself to lean more into growth rather than self-doubt.

In moments when anxiety feels overwhelming, it might seem impossible to live big or be brave. That's when the smallest acts become the most heroic. Taking one more breath, standing back up after a setback, seeking connection—these are all ways you're showing up stronger than anxiety expects. Bravery thrives in the cracks of difficulty, in the spaces where anxiety wants to stop you. By honoring these moments, you own your experience in a way that's real and sustainable.

Bravery can also grow through intention. By consciously deciding each day to redefine what bravery feels like for you, you build a foundation of self-trust and encouragement. When anxiety tries to rewrite the story with defeat, your inner voice, anchored in this new understanding, says: "I've got this." It's not about denying anxiety's presence but refusing to let it have the final word. Owning your days means owning your definition of brave—and that can change everything.

Sometimes, society's narrow definitions of bravery discourage people from asking for help. But part of living bigger than anxiety is recognizing that bravery is deeply social. It involves connection, community, and sometimes leaning on others. When you reach out or express your needs, you're showing a profound kind of courage—one that breaks down stigma and builds bridges. No one conquers anxiety completely alone, and recognizing that is a huge act of bravado in itself.

Finally, embracing this broader view of bravery won't make anxiety disappear overnight, nor will it erase the tough moments. But it does make a difference in how you experience those moments. Bravery becomes your ally, not a rigid expectation or an anxiety-triggering standard. It creates space for growth, resilience, and self-compassion—ingredients that help you own every day, no matter what comes.

Living bigger than anxiety asks you to see yourself through kinder eyes and honor the courage you practice daily. When you do, the idea of bravery transforms from a distant goal to a lived reality, fueling your journey with confidence and hope.

You're Not Broken— You're Building Something Stronger

As you reach this point, it's clear that anxiety doesn't define who you are. Those moments of panic, the overwhelming feelings swirling in your mind—they're not signs of failure or weakness. Instead, they're signals that your brain is working overtime, trying to protect you from perceived threats. What's truly remarkable is that experiencing anxiety doesn't mean you're broken. Far from it, you're crafting a stronger, more resilient version of yourself every day.

It's easy to fall into the trap of harsh self-judgment when anxiety steps in. You might feel like you're constantly battling a part of yourself, like an enemy hiding in plain sight. But this book has shown you that anxiety is more of an overzealous guardian than a destructive force. The tools you've learned weren't designed to "fix" you because there's nothing inherently wrong with you. Instead, these techniques act like guides, gently redirecting your brain's patterns and helping calm the storm.

That realization alone holds immense power. When you stop viewing yourself as broken, space opens up for healing. You begin to meet anxiety with kindness and curiosity rather than fear and frustration. This shift is at the heart of real transformation. The science behind what you've practiced—the quick 90-second resets, the breath work, the body awareness—reinforces one key truth: your brain is capable of change. It's plastic and adaptable, ready to rewire toward calm and control.

The path you're on isn't about quick fixes or magic formulas. It's about building strength through consistent practice and self-compassion. Change doesn't happen overnight, but every time you use the tools in this book, you're rewiring old habits. Each small victory chips away at the grip of anxiety's panic loop, making space for confidence to grow. Think of your journey like building a foundation. At first, progress might feel slow or invisible, but every brick you lay contributes to a stronger structure.

It's important to honor that strength already inside you. Anxiety can cloud your sense of self with doubt and criticism, but you've demonstrated courage by seeking understanding and taking action. Taking these steps requires more bravery than many realize. You've shown up, even on the days when it felt impossible. That's resilience in motion. You're not just surviving anxiety—you're learning to live beyond it.

Also, remember that setbacks don't erase the progress you've made. Anxiety tends to trick us into believing that a bad moment means failure. But growth is rarely linear. Sometimes you'll have tough days or sessions where the 90 seconds feel longer or less effective. That's completely normal.

Like any skill, mastery comes with patience and repeated effort. Each time you reset, reframe, or breathe through a wave of panic, you're reinforcing healthier pathways in your brain.

Another factor to keep in mind is that building strength is a deeply personal process. Your experience with anxiety is unique, and so is your healing journey. What feels right for someone else might not resonate with you—and that's okay. The value of this program lies in its flexibility, offering a menu of tools that fit different moments and moods. Experiment with these methods and trust your instincts on what helps you the most. Over time, you'll develop a toolkit uniquely yours, empowering you to take charge in any situation.

It's also worth recognizing the broader meaning of resilience—beyond simply stopping panic attacks. As you cultivate calm and control, you're building a mindset that carries into every part of your life. Anxiety may have limited your choices or dimmed your confidence before, but now you're reclaiming control. This new foundation offers a chance to reimagine what "brave" really means. It isn't about fearless perfection but showing up in spite of discomfort. It's the act of steady persistence and self-compassion rolled into one.

There's an undeniable beauty in this work: it transforms vulnerability into strength. Learning to manage anxiety invites you to get to know yourself on a deeper level. You may discover strengths you never realized you had—patience, empathy, adaptability. These qualities not only help you handle anxious moments but enrich your relationships and daily experiences. When you treat yourself with kindness during tough times, it teaches others how to support and respect you, too.

Moving forward, consider this journey as ongoing rather than complete. Life will always present stresses, surprises, and uncertainties. Anxiety might still visit occasionally, but you'll face those moments equipped with techniques grounded in science and proven by practice. The goal isn't to eliminate all discomfort—it's to change how you relate to it. By embracing this approach, you're increasing your mental flexibility and emotional resilience in a way that lasts.

Most importantly, celebrate the fact that you've already started building strength that many never do. Not everyone takes the time to learn about their anxiety, try actionable strategies, or commit to rewiring the brain. You're doing the hard work of growth, proving to yourself that you're more than any anxious episode. That's a profound accomplishment in itself, one worth recognizing every day.

In closing, you're not broken—not by any stretch. You're evolving into a more capable, aware, and empowered person. Each practice, pause, and breath brings you closer to owning your days on your terms. Keep trusting this process, stay patient with yourself, and remember: building something stronger isn't easy, but it's absolutely possible.

STOP ANXIETY NOW

You have everything you need within you to face anxiety with confidence and grace. And if ever doubt creeps in, remind yourself of the incredible progress you've made so far. You're not just reacting to anxiety—you're rebuilding your mind and life in a way that supports lasting calm and courage. Keep going, because your strength is growing with every step.

www.ingramcontent.com/pod-product-compliance
Lightning Source LLC
Chambersburg PA
CBHW032001080426

42735CB00007B/465